The American Assembly, *Columbia University*

PUBLIC WORKERS
AND PUBLIC UNIONS

Prentice-Hall, Inc., *Englewood Cliffs, N.J.*

A SPECTRUM BOOK

Current printing (last number):

10 9 8 7 6 5 4 3 2

PRENTICE-HALL INTERNATIONAL, INC. (*London*)
PRENTICE-HALL OF AUSTRALIA, PTY. LTD. (*Sydney*)
PRENTICE-HALL OF CANADA, LTD. (*Toronto*)
PRENTICE-HALL OF INDIA PRIVATE LIMITED (*New Delhi*)
PRENTICE-HALL OF JAPAN, INC. (*Tokyo*)

Preface

This book is intended to acquaint Americans with the realities of collective bargaining in federal, state, and local government.

In 1948 Henry M. Wriston, then president of Brown University, delivered an address in New York on the occasion of one of the first teachers' strikes in the nation, in Pawtucket, Rhode Island. He called the speech "Fire Bell in the Night!" In 1971 one of the writers of this volume discusses "our tolerance of civil disobedience . . . and our ability to adapt to various forms of disruption."

Whatever one's attitude toward these two views, the fact remains that the growth of public unions in recent years has been spectacular. Twenty-five percent of our governmental workers are now unionized. There exists therefore an urgent need for Americans to work creatively together to find ways of avoiding the pain and controversy which marked the progress of unionization in the private business and industrial sector.

As the report of the Fortieth American Assembly, *Collective Bargaining in American Government* (see below), points out, the the effect of broad, rapid growth of unions in government has been unsettling. Many public employers and public managers have been poorly prepared to understand or to deal with the new relationships. Many state and local governments are beginning to develop ground rules to help bring order out of the varied approaches to representation of employees; others have done nothing. Legislators have found some guidance from business and industry but have also discovered basic differences between public and private employment and have reflected this in their law-making.

A variety of approaches is emerging, some modified by the tests of time, others frankly enacted as hopeful experiments. Labor-management doctrine in private enterprise is being examined and challenged. So are prohibitions and practices in the public sector that existed before unions surfaced. Recognizing the mounting complexities of present and potential problems, editor Sam Zagoria designed this American Assembly volume to provide guidelines for strengthening the bargaining process and assuring its responsiveness to the public interest rather than wringing hands over strikes, slowdowns, and sick-outs and yearning for yesteryear. We expect that it will help.

Before appearing in public print the chapters which follow were used as background reading for participants at the Fortieth American Assembly, at Arden House, in the fall of 1971. The report of policy recommendations of

iii

that meeting may be had in pamphlet form from The American Assembly.

We are pleased that The Ford Foundation shared our sense of the importance of this public employment problem and contributed generous support for the entire national program, including the Arden House Assembly and a series of Assemblies around the nation. The Foundation, however, has nothing to do with the views expressed herein; those are the authors' own. And, of course, The American Assembly, as a nonprofit educational organization, takes no stand on matters it presents to the public.

Clifford C. Nelson
President
The American Assembly

Table of Contents

v

Introduction

In a nation honeycombed with communications media, where organizations watchdog trends for every conceivable interest, and public officials are expected to alert the nation on most everything every day, it is remarkable how little public attention has been given to a rising, unrelenting movement which will bring about more drastic renovation of government than a public administrator's most ambitious blueprint. Public unions, largely a phenomenon of the sixties, have experienced a boom in popularity and have burst upon public employers and a general public less prepared for them than for an invasion from outer space. Further, the speed of the changeover, measured against the backdrop of labor history, is almost breathtaking—public unions and employee associations have attracted a larger proportion of their share of the work force in 10 years than the industrial unions have been able to do in 30.

For years and years public workers accepted working terms and conditions offered by public management with equanimity, and generally speaking, they were good ones: merit hiring, broad fringe benefits, almost absolute job security, and an assured income (not dependent on vagaries of weather, availability of risk capital, or the ebb and flow of fads and fashions). In truth, these were the trade-offs for the private sector unionism.

But now we are going through a quiet revolution of government. Workers are not scaling the ramparts to overthrow our institutions,

SAM ZAGORIA is director of the Labor-Management Relations Service established by the National League of Cities, U.S. Conference of Mayors, and the National Association of Counties. He is a former member of the National Labor Relations Board and was previously administrative assistant to U.S. Senator Clifford P. Case and reporter for The Washington Post.

but they are effectively building some new passageways into the executive and council chambers where public policy is determined.

Public unions are not only sounding the traditional demand for "more," they are also seeking a greater voice in assuring proper working conditions and work loads, the making of job assignments, transfers and promotions, and at least consultation in reorganization of institutional structures. Public workers thus are edging into the governmental policy-planning and policy-making machinery. Some are quite plain about the ultimate objective—sharing of power.

To the public employer accustomed to making unilateral determinations in these and other matters, the idea of sharing power with his workers takes a little getting used to. Before, if he wanted to change working hours, he issued a bulletin and that was that. Before, if he thought a school class size of 35 was sound—educationally and economically—he directed it. Today he faces the possibility that such an assignment will be protested by a teacher as an intolerable working condition, and he faces the multiple steps of a grievance process culminating, perhaps, in an arbitrator ruling against him. And today's arbitration victory for one teacher may become the basis for a negotiation demand tomorrow on behalf of all the teachers in the system.

The collective bargaining process diminishes the decision-making powers of the public employer in other ways, too. As negotiated contracts raise personnel costs, shifts frequently must be made away from capital expenditures to operating budgets, or it may be that a wage settlement for policemen or firemen may force a reduction in the corps of sanitation workers. If a contract deadlock goes to third-party fact-finding or arbitration, the public employer knows that, as a practical matter, like it or not, he must accept the recommendation or award.

To say these things about the effect of the collective bargaining process is not to argue that it is contrary to the public interest. It has been national labor policy in the private sector for decades. Many public employers have found that the improvement in morale accomplished through giving employees a voice in their own destiny has far outweighed the strain and struggle of the negotiating table. Some have found that situations unfolded during negotiations or grievance handling have disclosed unfair or improper conduct that it was to the advantage of all concerned to remedy.

Public employers, taking their lead from public attitudes toward government unionism, have not been fighting unions. They may not have encouraged them but mostly they have accepted employee decisions on representation, except in those geographic areas where unions are still a dirty word—in public or private. In a few situations, public unions and public employers have even been accused of going too far in cooperating, using a private settlement to negate public policy.

The biggest success of public unions has come in local government. It has come at a time when state and federal governments generally have been talking about more power and funds for cities and counties. And the outlook is that for the remainder of this decade local government will be the major growth sector in the nation, so further union growth may be anticipated. The municipal labor-management relationship has been complicated by inexperience on both sides, substantial turnover in the nation's 15,000 mayors, a growing fiscal plight, and rising job aspirations of urban minorities.

In this book New York City receives a great deal of attention, partly because it has had long experience, has pioneered in a tripartite approach to labor relations, and also because it has reached almost the ultimate in unionization. Already 205,000 of the city's eligible 210,000 employees are represented; presently $12 million a year is deducted from employee checks by the city for union dues; by 1980, the city's work force is expected to reach 500,000 and if the same ratio of union membership prevails, the city unions collectively will be larger than most of the internationals in the AFL-CIO. While other cities are not as union-oriented—public and private—there are those who feel that whatever happens in Big City, USA, is bound to happen first in New York City and on a large scale. New York City stands as an interesting case history and as a clue to what may therefore be occurring in many cities in years to come.

Federal government administrators, mandated by three executive orders, conditioned by a major postal strike and a paralyzing air controllers' sickout, are also finding out about collective bargaining. Previously Congress decided all pay and fringe issues, and the Civil Service Commission took care of the rest. But now federal administrators, long kings in their own departments, are finding that 58 percent of their employees are represented by unions and it's a whole new ball game.

Public employers—federal, state, and local—accustomed to administering employee relations "by the book" are learning that with collective bargaining there are now two sides to deal with the rules, and "papa knows best" homilies can be relegated to the home for the aged.

While much has been written comparing public to private sector unionism, one essential difference divides them—the prohibition of strikes against the government. A few nibbles have been taken at granting the right to strike in a few jurisdictions, but for the most part, the public worker strike is still legally prohibited. Nonetheless it is happening—some would accept it as inevitable and necessary to the bargaining process and legalize it; others are concentrating on perfecting impasse-resolution machinery as a substitute and some are focusing on how to enforce strike penalties without impeding dispute settlements. On one position there is general agreement—we need to find ways to achieve more respect for law and save public servants from the anomalous position of violating laws they are committed to uphold.

The issues raised by this new wave of unionism are examined here by a group of practitioners, observers, and participants. After a decade of fast growth the authors have found it useful to sit back and reflect on their experiences. Each has been encouraged to address himself with frankness to his assigned topic. The close reader will find that the authors do not always agree with one another and indeed occasionally deposit some bundles of blame at the door of a writing colleague. None, except the editor, I might add, has had the opportunity to see another's product in advance so the lack of a reply to a charge does not necessarily mean no response was possible.

With these caveats, the editor wishes readers a pleasant and instructive exposure to the joys and frustrations of collective bargaining in government.

John W. Macy, Jr.

1

The Role of Bargaining
in the Public Service

Inadequate Attention

Public employment at all levels of government has been the recent growth factor in the American labor market. National unions have identified the extension of union membership in public service as a primary objective. Public service strikes involving teachers, sanitation workers, hospital attendants, firemen, and policemen have increasingly dominated the labor relations news in the country. And yet, the citizen and his elected representatives in government have devoted far too little attention to the role of unions in the public service. While the citizen is the beneficiary of the public employee's performance and the financial supporter of the public employee's wages and benefits, his voice has been confused or muted in the formulation of public policy on government's relations with these workers.

To a decided degree the complexity and magnitude of public employment have frustrated the citizen's understanding of labor relations in the public sector. The growth, diversity, and size of public employment defy ready understanding. Public employees are present in every community in every conceivable type of job, but they are on the payrolls of different governmental entities—federal, state, regional, county, district, municipal, and even quasi-governmental organizations. In fact, with the performance of government services

JOHN W. MACY, JR. *is president of the Corporation for Public Broadcasting. He was a federal career employee for more than twenty years, executive vice president of Wesleyan University, and chairman of the United States Civil Service Commission under Presidents Kennedy and Johnson. In 1969 he was awarded the Presidential Medal of Freedom.*

5

under contract or grant, many private enterprises are significantly
financed and their employees paid with public dollars. Private corpora-
tions with public service functions and regulated by public agencies
perform essential services parallel to those of government. The line between the public and the private sector has become increasingly
blurred, with resulting confusion compounded in the determination of
labor relations policies.

In the past, this public policy issue has been the subject of attention
on the part of experts, academicians, or those directly engaged in the
process. Far too many public officials with legislative and executive responsibility have handed off this hot potato to consultants or advisers
removed from both direct responsibility and direct exposure to the
issue. When the emerging problems erupted in crisis form, policies and
processes were adopted under pressure and were not necessarily reflec-
tive of the public interest nor designed to achieve long-term solutions.

HIGH ON POLICY AGENDA

Before discussing the role of bargaining in the public service and
thereby joining the ranks of the consultants and advisers, I would
strongly urge that each and every public jurisdiction place this issue
high on its agenda for executive study and for legislative review. Even
the most forward-looking and well-balanced policy is not adequate to
the future resolution of the problems bound to arise in this public
area of sensitivity and significance. This is not an issue which is susceptible to uniform treatment across the country even in jurisdictions of
like form and purpose. It is not an issue which should carry partisan
political markings. The unique characteristics of each community and
each jurisdiction are such that case-by-case study and action are required. This is an issue on which general principles and broad guidance can be useful but where the decision making must ultimately be
made within the context of each unit of government.

Circumstances of Public Service Unions

To consider the role of public service unions it is necessary to
study the stage on which they must perform and the other actors with
whom they must interact. The stage may resemble the setting of any
other employment situation, but it is basically different. Democratic
government and public interest make that setting distinctive and, in
truth, significantly influence the course of the drama in the roles of
the other actors.

PUBLIC INTEREST IS PARAMOUNT

Without engaging in complex discourse about political philosophy
and constitutional traditions, the relationship of employer and em-

ployee in the public context must start with the fundamental premise that the public interest is paramount. The function or mission performed by the public employee was judged by a legislative body to be essential for the public welfare and safety. The management responsible for the performance of these functions and missions is accountable to that legislative body and ultimately to the people. The administrative processes and standards devised by management for the delivery of these services are subject to the scrutiny of elected officials. This management is not a free agent in the employment of men and women whose skills and capabilities are the ultimate means by which the public receives the legislatively intended service. Management's discretion is specified and curbed by both the legislative determinations and the administrative judgments of regulatory and supervisory executive agencies, such as personnel or financial management organizations. In certain areas these restrictions narrow the discretion of successive levels of managers to the point where their decision making with respect to employment matters is confined to applying the policies in the rule book or performing certain clerical rituals.

BALANCE OF BENEFITS AND OBLIGATIONS

When an American accepts employment on a public payroll he knowingly or unknowingly accepts certain special conditions which have been judged necessary by a combination of legislative, executive, and judicial decisions. Although the nature of his task, the content of his workday, and the extent of his responsibility may vary little or not at all from that of an employee in the private sector, the mere fact that his employment is *public* alters his working conditions. He is afforded certain special benefits or protections—civil service tenure, assurance against arbitrary dismissal, nondiscriminatory selection in hiring, promoting and receiving training—and he must accept certain obligations and restrictions—rigid pay schedules, fixed qualification standards, employment investigations, security and classification limitations, and, in some cases, prohibition against political activity and restrictions on his freedom to deny his service. Through the evolution of American public service, a balance of these benefits and obligations, protections and prohibitions has been sought in the face of ever changing conditions. And at best it is an imperfect balance which is constantly subject to adjustment through new legislative or executive actions, through pressure from employees individually and collectively, through court decisions, and through changing public awareness. The growth of bargaining in the public service has been generated to some degree by the existence of this balance and the necessity for its continuing adjustment. The growth has been accelerated in many jurisdictions because of a conviction on the part of the employees that imbalance existed and that collective action and more effective representation of employees was necessary to bring about change or to accelerate improvement.

But these special conditions of public service do not argue in favor of isolation of union-management relations in the public sector from all experience and practice in the private realm. Not at all. The development of the labor movement in government closely parallels and is frequently a part of the history of the labor movement in its relations with the corporate world. Many of the characteristics, favorable and unfavorable, found in the private sector are evident among government unions—craft versus industrial rivalry, national versus local representation, maintenance of membership, financing of union activities, discipline within the union. Likewise, many of the processes which have been devised through bargaining and dispute have become directly applicable in the public arena—the definition of unit, the form of recognition, the patterns of grievance resolution, the processes of negotiation. In fact, many international unions include substantial representations of public as well as private employees.

LAGGARD POLICY ACTION

In the past 40 years of rising union-management relations in this country, the leaders in the public service have been laggard in establishing policies and conditions for effective relationships between employee groups and public managers. Even in the New Deal years when labor relations became a topic of active national interest and when federal leadership moved to establish by statute policies and machinery to govern the private sector in this area, little serious attention was given to government's own relations with the labor unions. Franklin Roosevelt while expressing pride in the Wagner Act could only speak in restrictive terms to the unions within the federal government. Restrictive attitudes of this type toward unionization of government were even more prevalent and forcefully expressed at the local levels. It should be recognized, therefore, that philosophy and doctrine with respect to public labor relations is still in the formative stage but can no longer be neglected by those who have responsibility for public programs.

In searching for historical reasons to explain delay in the development of public labor relations policy it is difficult to be definitive. There undoubtedly has been a prevalent tendency to believe that the government as sovereign could not negotiate with its own employees. There has also been the historical development of the civil service concept in public employment. This concept was articulated and applied to move government employment out of political activity and to give the employee and the public an assurance of equal opportunity and merit competition in seeking and holding a public position. The civil service concept placed heavy emphasis on the individual and on the rights and benefits related to the employee individually and not to group action or decision.

INCOMPATIBILITY WITH CIVIL SERVICE

For many years it was almost an article of faith among government practitioners that there was a fundamental incompatibility between the civil service concept and collective bargaining. The conventional wisdom was that the standards of individual merit would clash with the traditional aspects of collective action and more particularly with certain maintenance of membership practices. Some elements of incompatibility do in fact exist, but contemporary needs call for an innovative pattern of relationships between the two so that the benefits of both systems may be available to management, unions, and the public. Such an objective has been the goal of study groups, legislative bodies, and labor relations practitioners in these times. That objective was inherent in the statements of labor relations policy and practice enunciated in the executive orders issued by President Kennedy in 1962 and President Nixon in 1969 for the federal service. As state and local governments formulated policy positions they too followed this objective.

THE ROLE OF THE LEGISLATURE

Another reason for retarded development of public labor relations policy was the important role in many jurisdictions played by the legislative body. As public unions were organized in the earlier years of the century their collective target was more likely to be the federal Congress, the state legislature, or the city council rather than the executive officials. The rise in pay, the addition of a new leave benefit, the shortening of working hours, the introduction of group health and life insurance programs were all to be secured through the action of the people's representatives. Because those representatives were sensitive to public opinion and were accessible to representatives of ever larger groups, why should union representatives devote time and energy in lobbying or negotiating with public executives? Union power could be focused with far greater effectiveness upon sympathetic and responsive elected officials than upon the managers with whom they dealt in the regular employee-employer relationship.

To some degree this power pattern has been altered in recent times as legislative bodies tended to limit their policy setting to broad statements of public intent and delegated increasing amounts of discretion to executive officials. As a result of these delegations, public executives have found more and more collective bargaining opportunities, and union participation in decision making with respect to pay, benefits, and working conditions has been brought close to the traditional private model. But legislative bodies will continue to be an important factor in the planning of the role of bargaining in the public service. Many legislators will be reluctant to give up their own part in settling the bread and butter issues of labor relations, and in any event they control the ultimate power in the appropriation of funds to convert agreements into dollars in the pay envelope or the pension fund. All too frequently the critics in this field have failed to give adequate weight to the importance of these elected officials in the bargaining process. Even if they are not at the table their presence is a strong though invisible force in any public bargaining.

DIFFERENCES BETWEEN PUBLIC AND PRIVATE SECTORS

This is in sharp contrast to the situation that prevails in private employment and serves as an appropriate introduction to the consideration of the decided differences that do exist. These differences need to be understood because one obstacle in the search for effective solutions in public service labor relations is disagreement on the question of whether government service is essentially different from private employment. In any public jurisdiction, unless all of the organizations can accept the existence of this difference, the road of labor-management relations will be too perilous for the public to travel. The government involved and the public which supports it will be too suspicious of unionism to permit it to play its proper and important role in public service. Conversely, if the government and the public it serves believe that the union recognizes and accepts the essential difference, then all of the problems of equality of status, methods of operation, and particular aspects of the relationship have a good chance of resolution. There are many areas of difference but three of them are important in gaining an understanding.

First, in private enterprise authority is located clearly at the top of the corporate organization. The subordinate organization and delegations of authority usually are clearly drawn and the scope and magnitude of responsibility in labor relations can be defined with a reasonable degree of precision. In democratic governments, on the other hand, ultimate authority is at the base rather than at the top of the structure. The citizens themselves elect their representatives, define their authority within constitutional limits, and provide internal checks and balances or oversight to insure that the will of the majority prevails in decision making.

This difference in the location of basic authority, and the way in which operating authority is limited and diffused within the ranks of government, is a focal point in many of the complications that exist in public service labor relations. Unions are inclined to complain about their inability to deal, as in private enterprise, directly with the source of "yes" or "no" final authority. This attitude denies a reality which cannot be changed. The same attitude is frequently evident in the impatience of the public with the delay on the part of public management in the resolution of issues relating to union demands.

The second difference lies in the way in which management authority actually is exercised in government. While government leaders do have defined authority to act as management, the nature of their action is strongly affected by the need to weigh and balance divergent interests of major groups among the citizens they represent. In many instances a union dispute far transcends the issue of pay or benefits or working conditions in a public program. At stake may be essential services the denial of which will set off a chain of crippling consequences. For example, in the 1968 teachers' dispute in New York City where the public schools were closed for many weeks, 52,000 teachers denied their services to the schools, and the lives of more than a million schoolchildren and their parents were deeply affected. This dispute did not relate to pay or other economic issues. To the union, the issue was job security, protection of the working rights of its members. But to the city government and the school board, the issue was considerably broader. The parties in confrontation were not just labor and management; they included many other groups representing educational, civic, political, racial, and religious interests. So the real issue is one of public policy—in this case, public educational policy, a policy so fundamental to the welfare of the community that it was surrounded by a mixture of pressures, politics, and prejudice of such complexity as to obstruct any resolution through traditional dealings between the union and management.

Third, the process of public policy formulation is frequently responsible for many of the working conditions specified for public employees. These conditions may be regarded as uniquely different or perhaps less beneficial than those in private business. No amount of pressure for change brought by an employee union will influence such a policy. In fact, labor relations may receive an unjustified black eye for a public position unrelated to labor-management negotiations. For example, the policy decision to decentralize the school system in New York created conditions which promoted the teachers' dispute outside of normal labor relations. Likewise, the federal air traffic controllers' complaints concerning work practices transcended union issues and related to policy decisions on control of air traffic. The task of resolving questions of public policy is the task of government and should not be a burden borne by a labor-management relationship even if deterioration in that relationship serves to draw public attention to the questions requiring resolution.

NEEDED ACCEPTANCE OF DIFFERENCES

These essential differences between public service and private employment need to be accepted by all parties to public service labor relations. These differences need to be reflected in attitudes and approaches to these relationships. This does not mean in any sense that the role of labor unions in public service should be more limited than in private employment just because the role of management must be more limited. Instead it means that the test of labor success should not be recorded in terms of the forms and techniques of collective bargaining in the private sector, but in terms of similar results for the worker through whatever form of representation is best suited to the public jurisdiction involved. Form and technique should fit the authority and organizational pattern of the parties in the working setting. Labor relations arrangements properly differ not only between private industry and government but from one government to another. Where there is good experience that can be transferred from one setting to another, that may prove beneficial, but the main effort should be to develop forms of representation that are best suited to the actual circumstances existing in each public domain. There are significant opportunities to develop creative new patterns to meet the needs of public organizations in public programs independent of prototypes that may exist in industry or in other units of government.

BLURRED LINE BETWEEN MANAGEMENT AND UNIONS

Employee group activity in government has complicated and retarded the natural development of trade unions along the lines of industrial models. A personnel policy which emphasized freedom of choice on the part of the employees and permitted the formation of groups of all types tended to produce fractional groups with a great variety of interests. Employees are "free to join or refrain from joining" any organization designed for their well-being and not contrary to the public interest—so read many a public employment policy for many years. Groups of all types were formed where the cohesive factor was previous military service, church affiliation, hobby interests, professional development, or shared recreational interests. While management did not overtly encourage these groups it provided sympathy and facilities which fostered their multiplication. Union organization has occurred over and around these activities in a crazy-quilt pattern of affiliation built on organizational lines, professional fields, craft and trade occupations, some with membership limited to government ranks, others associated with unions primarily for the industrial world. Both union and nonunion groups were concerned with various aspects of employment conditions. Out of this diversity in patterns of representation the recognition of units tended to create more rational relationships for meaningful employee-management cooperation. The mere definition of a union organization has posed a policy problem in many public jurisdictions.

But the definition of management has proved even more difficult to specify. Bargaining serves little purpose unless those representing management have a true sense of managerial commitment and authority to represent the managerial position in negotiations with responsible union leaders. Management representatives have been designated to negotiate at levels far removed from the point of ultimate decision with respect to basic issues. All too frequently the management negotiator has had a greater psychological affinity to the objectives of the union than to the distant and frequently ill-defined goals of management. To further complicate the roles in the bargaining drama, higher-paid supervisory personnel have often been union members and even spokesmen. In some governmental institutions, such as the Postal Service (formerly Post Office Department), relatively high-level supervisors and managers have formed organizations which behave in very much the same manner as employee unions. These associations have even sought recognition and certainly have engaged in well financed lobbying efforts in support of favorable legislation.

This behavioral history has blurred the line between union and management. It has frequently thwarted the development of orderly negotiation and in situations of growing tension has forced the formulation of expedient processes of resolution on the basis of political necessity.

PARTNERSHIP FOR BETTER COMMUNICATION

The portion of the public labor relations iceberg visible to the public usually appears loaded with dispute on gut issues involving large numbers of employees in publicly sensitive activities with substantial impact on the normal ways of public service. Critical as these conditions may be there is a much larger area of activity below the surface where sound labor-management relations operate on a daily basis to facilitate the conduct of public business, to improve employment conditions, and to resolve local grievances. These affirmative benefits which prevail in the great majority of governmental locations are testimony to the benefits gained from the painstaking formulation of policies and processes interrelating the two essential elements. These relationships afford a channel of communication and consultation which can never be achieved through the normal supervisory structure or through employee organizations built on other than employee representation bases. Through these peaceful processes extended efforts should be applied to elevate the quality of service delivered to the citizen and to be more effectively responsible to the needs of the public. In this fashion labor-management actions of an affirmative nature can remove the curse of irresponsible and unauthorized actions which leave the taxpayer as the true victim. Wildcat strikes, misuse of sick leave, intentional disruption of public transportation or sanitation collection not only produce community distress but will ultimately provoke a taxpayers' revolt against those employed to serve them.

NEGLECTED WORKING CONDITIONS

It cannot be denied that executive and legislative failure to recognize the essential needs of employees have increased the appeal of union action, both responsible and irresponsible. In all too many jurisdictions management has accepted the popular myth that public service deserved a lesser reward than private employment or, worse still, that low pay could be supplemented through petty graft or chiseling. The physical plant and working conditions have often been substandard. There have been as many loft buildings and World War Two temporaries occupied by government workers as there have been marble monuments and modern office buildings. Health and safety programs have frequently been deficient. While some benefits may have been generous, others have been nonexistent. Programs with limited political visibility or of necessity performed in undesirable neighborhoods have not received the management attention they deserve. On top of these deficiencies there has been the perpetual drive to restrain the ever rising costs of government and to score political points through alleged reductions in payroll expenses. While increased union demand and the institution of regular bargaining may have increased employee costs, the resulting improvement in conditions should produce greater productivity and better public service.

Fundamental Policies, Standards, and Processes

Although it is dangerous to generalize in defining an environment for constructive labor-management relations at all levels of government, certain fundamental principles, standards and processes can be outlined for the guidance of parties seeking effective resolution.

Declaration of Basic Policy—There should be a clear declaration of executive and legislative policy enunciating the right of public employees to join unions. It is strange that in the last third of the twentieth century in the United States it is still necessary to offer this assertion. But many local jurisdictions have failed to state this basic right until forced to do so under the pressure of an escalating dispute.

Patterns of Representation—This right must be accompanied by delineation of representation patterns which can serve as an effective means of communication between management and employees. This forms the basis for a limited partnership where both parties willingly accept certain specified rights and obligations. Without these representation rights the labor-management relationship in public employment is hollow and negligible and the public service benefits of the relationship cannot be achieved.

Democratic Selection of Union Representation—Systematic processes should be developed whereby employees in a predetermined and well defined unit can choose by democratic action the union they wish to have represent them. When a majority of the unit employees designate a particular union, management should recognize that union as the exclusive employee representative in the unit. To permit the union to perform its basic function as advocate for its members, management must recognize that the union speaks for all employees in communications or negotiations with the employer. The steps leading to union recognition should be adapted to fit the specific conditions. Although there is substantial debate over the definition of the most desirable unit, public employment generally has been best served through the largest feasible unit for recognition consistent with acceptable negotiation conditions. Ordinarily this will help to avoid potential distortion in public services which can occur when negotiations are conducted by one government agency with a particular unit without regard for negotiation by other agencies under the same governmental authority. By the same token it can be argued that too broad a unit will fail to give appropriate attention to specialized working situations in particular operating programs or occupations. Broadened units will also avoid the creation or preservation of separate units based on racial or ethnic lines. In the past certain public employers have been unwilling to grant recognition because of outstanding questions about a given union's standing or capability or because of anticipated demands that may be brought on by recognition in excess of their ability to finance. These reservations must be overcome if a policy is to exist which acknowledges the representativeness of a union which has gained the majority will.

Obligation to Negotiate in Good Faith—Both parties must accept an obligation to meet and negotiate in good faith within a reasonable time after recognition has been granted. Before negotiations are opened the scope of issues to be covered should be precisely defined in order to avoid to the maximum extent possible potential disagreement over permissible areas. It is necessary for the public employer to reserve certain management rights relating to organization and program, and in many instances certain topics of negotiation may be excluded by preemption of the legislative body. Nevertheless, the public manager should not exclude from consultation and discussion issues judged to be significant by union representatives even if negotiations are prohibited. In several jurisdictions management has been reluctant to broaden the scope of issues to be negotiated with union representatives; more affirmative benefits to both parties have been secured when management has demonstrated a willingness to extend the range of issues open to discussion.

Comprehensive and Precise Agreements—The results of negotiation should be promptly recorded and distributed throughout the unit. The composition of agreements is often a long and painful experience but once it is achieved it provides the basic foundation on which further relationships can be constructed. In labor relations, processes are almost as important as substance. This should not be overlooked in the drafting of the agreement. Many a controversy can be sparked by obscure references to the processes to be followed in resolving disputes.

Effective Grievance Machinery—At the core of most agreements should be the design of the grievance machinery. That mechanism should contain the necessary provisions for final settlement by impartial arbitration. Experience has demonstrated that a more affirmative relationship is formed when a mutually agreed upon complaint process is negotiated. Otherwise, grievances may be allowed to fester by inattentive management before an equitable decision is reached. The lack of this machinery can easily lead to disputes because employees have no alternative methods of pressing their claim against existing or imagined unfair treatment. This is particularly significant in the public sector where grievances can arise out of the nature of the work and the degree of contact with the citizens. There may be a reluctance on the part of management to permit the outside arbitrator to render a binding decision on a grievance in a sensitive and unfamiliar public program. Arbitration may serve as a useful means in carrying the grievance outside of the management hierarchy where employees believe that successive levels of supervision will only support the original management judgment. But the record in both public and private employment has shown that as long as these settlements are within the scope of legal authority and are subject to ultimate review by the courts, the manager will not be seriously handicapped and in most instances will be affirmatively relieved by this procedure.

Process for Impasse Settlement—When an impasse does arise, again previously agreed upon procedures should be applied. It is in this area of policy where public employment necessitates the construction of a process which will be pursued by both parties in the resolution of a dispute as an alternative to the employee work stoppage or the management lockout. It would not be accurate to attribute the rising number of public employee work stoppages to deficiencies in dispute resolution processes. In many instances, the specified process has not been followed and court injunctions or penalties have been imposed or politically enforced settlements have been consummated. Failure to follow the process and subsequent difficulties may justifiably be attributed to lack of experience on the part of both union and management representatives during the early stages of formal relations. Where experience has been gained and benefits recognized by both parties secured, these difficulties decline in frequency.

Alternatives to the strike as a means of settling disputes must be established for all agencies of government. This flat statement will be disputed by many who claim that strikes in the public service are basically no more threatening than strikes in certain industries. In offering this assertion there are frequently reservations with respect to the right to strike of firemen and policemen and others concerned with the health and safety of the community. It is contended that public employees should be permitted to strike if government authority with the decision-making power fails to accept the recommendation handed down through the dispute settlement procedure.

The contrary view is that employees should work on the terms negotiated, follow the dispute settlement procedure, seek redress through legislative authority, and be barred from striking by law. In this view it is contended that a blanket prohibition should apply to any and all public employees, that distinctions are difficult to draw, and that public service to the taxpayers cannot be disrupted. It is plain that government workers are employees of the public at large, acting through elected legislators, who may delegate but not abdicate certain authority to administrative officials. In accepting government employment, the employees have committed themselves to public service not to be interrupted by dissatisfaction over working conditions. Permitting strikes disrupts the functioning of government even if the functions performed by the employees can be defined as nonessential.

Though it may be increasingly unpopular these days this latter view is more persuasive, provided that the previously cited principles are established and pursued in good faith by both parties. If the prohibitory statute is violated, prescribed penalties must be assessed with firmness and fairness without creating martyrs of the leaders or imposing undue economic sanctions on the members. Certain existing statutes impose such onerous penalties that courts and administrative officials have virtually refused to impose them. The more appropriate penalties should be those involving the union's relationship with management, such as the suspension of recognition or the denial of the privilege of dues withholding. Such penalties are relevant to the violation of the negotiation process and have serious consequences for the offending leaders. The economic significance of checkoff cannot be overestimated. It is the lifeblood of the union's strength and the force in its political leverage. Its loss will seriously handicap its ability to represent its members during the period of suspension.

But what of the process by which these threatened disputes may be resolved? Initially, they should be exposed to intensified and continuing negotiations between all parties until the prospect of agreement is exhausted. At that point, the techniques of mediation can be introduced in seeking new forms of discussion on the part of the disputing parties. Basically, this mediation is intended to avert the breakdown of communication between parties and the abandonment of the effort to secure ultimate understanding. It injects into the controversy an outside neutral force to preside over what has escalated to an unresolvable dispute. It is essential that the mediator be acceptable to both parties and that he possess professional qualifications for dealing with the particular issue faced by the governmental organization involved.

If mediation fails, the next step should be the process of fact-finding performed by a public official or by a separate board established for this purpose. This process should be flexible and left open to those selected to manage it. The results of the fact-finding effort should provide the basis for resumed negotiation with the ultimate yielding on the part of one party or the other, or both parties, in a final agreement. Beyond fact-finding the agreement may call for an outside arbitrator to provide either advisory or binding decisions with respect to the issues of the dispute. Parties are reluctant to include this ultimate third-party decision making in the dispute settlement procedure. But such arbitrary action is preferable to the use of the ultimate weapon—the work stoppage. Only a relatively small number of cases should fail resolution with the completion of these steps of negotiation, mediation, and fact-finding and deteriorate into a strike situation.

Agency to Monitor Performance—The importance of the role of bargaining in the public service calls for the creation of an agency within the governmental framework at each jurisdictional level to oversee and evaluate it. In most jurisdictions an agency independent of executive action and subject only to court review is the most desirable model. This agency should monitor the compliance by both parties with basic principles of the program. It should periodically report to the public on the manner in which these relationships have been conducted in carrying out a jointly developed code of fair practices in public service labor relations.

Public Sector May Take the Lead

These have been years of rapid change in government programs. The increase in demands for public education, the awareness of need for broader social services, the drive to halt environmental deterioration, the concern over law enforcement and public safety, these and many other public objectives have imposed new burdens upon public administration. Disillusion and frustration with government have been found in many quarters ranging from the President himself to the representatives of the counterculture. High expectations of drastic social change have been dashed by the failure of government machinery and people to deliver the expected services. In the midst of these tensions new patterns of labor-management relations have been formulated. No ideal prescription can be formulated for installation in the more than thirty thousand public jurisdictions. But these relationships are essential to the ongoing change required in public service. The evolving role of bargaining can be beneficial or destructive. Administrators, labor leaders, legislators, and voters must turn their creative attention to this relationship in order to assure the beneficial result. Descriptions and assessments of successful experiences should be widely disseminated. Candid criticism of failures should be studied for clues leading to new approaches. More and more, the strike is viewed as a questionably effective economic weapon even in the private sector. Why should it increasingly become the symptom of failure in the public sector? It may well be that the demanding challenge to find improved relationships in the public sector may establish new patterns in responsible peace-making machinery where the balance of justice and fairness to the employee and responsive service to the public may be maintained in constructive equilibrium.

Lee C. Shaw*

2

The Development of State and Federal Laws

Background

The most important single development in labor relations in the United States in the past decade has been the advent of widespread public employee unionism. At a time when private sector unions were largely stagnating, unions representing public employees grew at an unprecedented rate. During the 1960s the number of public employees who belonged to unions and associations more than doubled, increasing from a little over 1 million in 1960 to 2.2 million in 1968. Among individual unions the rate of growth was even greater. The American Federation of State, County, and Municipal Employees (AFSCME) expanded its membership from 185,000 in 1960 to 460,000 in 1970. In 1964 it was the nineteenth largest affiliate in the AFL-CIO; in early 1970 it was the seventh largest. The American Federation of Government Employees (AFGE) saw its membership increase from 70,000 in 1960 to 325,000 in 1970. Symbolic of the steadily increasing role of public employee unions in the American labor movement was the recent addition of Jerry Wurf, president of AFSCME, and John Griner, president of AFGE, to the prestigious Executive Council of the AFL-CIO.

LEE C. SHAW *is a partner in Seyfarth, Shaw, Fairweather and Geraldson, a Chicago law firm representing private and public managements. Author of many articles on labor problems, he has been a consultant to three presidential administrations, including the current one, on labor relations.*

* Mr. Shaw acknowledges the assistance of R. Theodore Clark, Jr., a partner with the same law firm.

This tremendous growth in public employee unionism has been both the cause and effect of significant changes in the legal climate surrounding the rights and obligations of public employees and public employers alike, as well as in the virtual onslaught of legislation that has been passed at the federal, state, and local level concerning public employee labor relations. In this chapter the author intends to trace the legal and legislative developments that have occurred in the past ten years and to discuss the significant trends.

Judicial Developments

RIGHT TO JOIN AND FORM UNIONS

Prior to 1960, the courts with near unanimity held that public employees did not have any constitutional right to join or form unions and, as a corollary to this principle, that legislative bodies could affirmatively forbid their employees from joining and forming some or all unions. As late as 1963 the Michigan Supreme Court upheld in *AFSCME, Local 201 v. City of Muskegon,* the constitutionality of a regulation adopted by the chief of police of the City of Muskegon that prohibited any of the police officers employed by the city from becoming a member of any organization in any manner identified with any labor union or federation that admitted to membership persons who were not members of the Muskegon Police Department. The court noted that "there is no provision of either State or Federal Constitution which gives to individuals the right to be employed in government service or the right to continue therein."

In 1968 the United States Court of Appeals for the Seventh Circuit (Illinois, Indiana, Wisconsin) held for the first time in *McLaughlin v. Tilendis* that "an individual's right to form and join a union is protected by the First Amendment." This landmark case involved two teachers who instituted suit against a local school district alleging that their teaching contracts had not been renewed because of their activities on behalf of the American Federation of Teachers. In finding that their right to join and form a union fell within the ambit of the First Amendment, the court noted that "the Civil Rights Act of 1871 gives them a remedy if their contracts were not renewed because of their exercise of constitutional rights."

Subsequently, several other courts of appeal have likewise held that public employees have a First Amendment right to join and form unions. Moreover, state statutes in at least two states which prohibited all or certain categories of public employees from joining unions have been declared unconstitutional. The trend toward greater judicial protection of the right of public employees to join and form unions is clear and unmistakable.

RIGHT TO BARGAIN IN ABSENCE OF LEGISLATION

While public employees have a constitutional right to join and form unions, the courts have uniformly held that there is no constitutional right to force a public employer to bargain collectively in the absence of legislation. Thus, the Seventh Circuit, in a decision issued subsequent to *McLaughlin,* succinctly stated that "there is no constitutional duty to bargain collectively with an exclusive bargaining agent. Such duty when imposed is imposed by statute" (*Indianapolis Education Association v. Lewallen,* 1969).

Apart from constitutional considerations, the courts have repeatedly had to decide whether a public employer, in the absence of legislation, has the authority to bargain collectively and to enter into a written collective bargaining agreement. Up to the mid 1960s, the courts by and large held that public employers, especially when acting in a governmental capacity, did not have the authority to bargain collectively in the absence of legislation specifically authorizing it. Recently, however, there has been a distinct trend toward holding that a public employer, in the absence of legislation, has the authority to voluntarily engage in collective bargaining. Representative of these latter cases is *Chicago Division of the Illinois Education Association v. Board of Education of the City of Chicago* (1966), where the Illinois Appellate Court held that the Chicago Board of Education did "not require legislative authority to enter into a collective bargaining agreement with a sole collective bargaining agency selected by its teachers and . . . that such an agreement is not against public policy."

RIGHT TO STRIKE

No question has dominated discussions of public sector labor relations more than the question whether some or all categories of public employees should be allowed to strike. Not surprisingly, the question has repeatedly been presented to the courts, and the courts with near uniformity have held that public employees do not have the right to strike. Similarly the courts have repeatedly held that there is no constitutional right to strike and that strikes by public employees can be legislatively proscribed. In a 1971 case involving a broad frontal attack on the constitutionality of the federal statute prohibiting federal employees from participating in a strike (*Postal Clerks v. Blount*), the United States District Court for the District of Columbia stated:

> Given the fact that there is no constitutional right to strike, it is not irrational or arbitrary for the Government to condition employment on a promise not to withhold labor collectively, and to prohibit strikes by those in public employment, whether because of the prerogatives of the sovereign, some sense of higher obligation associated with public service, to as-

sure the continuing functioning of the Government without interruption, to protect public health and safety, or other reasons.

Concomitant with the proposition that strikes by public employees are illegal is the proposition that public employers can obtain injunctions against such rights. The mere fact that a public employee strike is enjoined, however, does not mean that the public employees and their union will obey the injunction. Indeed, the open defiance by many public sector unions of lawfully issued injunctions against strikes is one of the most pressing and disturbing problems in public sector labor relations today.

Despite the near uniformity of court decisions prohibiting strikes by public employees, one development deserves mention. The Michigan Supreme Court in *Holland v. Holland Education Ass'n* (1968) apparently carved out a significant exception to the generally accepted proposition that all strikes by public employees are enjoinable. The court refused to affirm an injunction issued by the trial court against a teacher strike in the absence of a showing of violence, irreparable injury, or breach of the peace. While the *Holland* decision is significant in that it departs from prior precedent, it should be noted that it represents the approach of only one state. The overwhelming majority viewpoint is that public employee strikes are enjoinable *without* any showing of irreparable harm. Since Michigan is the only state to adopt such an approach, the *Holland* decision cannot be said to constitute a trend.

Legislative Developments

While there were many significant legal developments during the 1960s, of greater significance has been the virtual onslaught of legislation concerning public employee labor relations. Prior to 1960, only one state, Wisconsin in 1959, had enacted comprehensive legislation that gave public employees a legally enforceable right to bargain collectively and the federal government had not yet acted in this area. Since 1960, however, Presidents Kennedy and Nixon have each issued an executive order; Congress has passed the Postal Reorganization Act; and over 30 states have enacted reasonably comprehensive legislation covering some or all categories of public employees. By use of the term "reasonably comprehensive legislation," we mean legislation that generally provides a method for resolving questions concerning representation, prohibits public employers and/or unions from engaging in unfair labor practices, sets forth procedures to deal with collective bargaining impasses, and establishes a public employee relations board (PERB) to administer the act. An analysis of the major provisions of these executive orders and legislative acts follows.

EXECUTIVE ORDERS 10988 AND 11491

It would be hard to exaggerate the major significance which President Kennedy's promulgation of Executive Order 10988 on January 17, 1962, has had on public employee labor relations in this country. Executive Order 10988 marked for the first time recognition by the federal government that its employees had the right to join and form unions and bargain collectively. The order provided for three separate forms of recognition—exclusive, formal, and informal—depending upon the percentage of employees which the labor organization represented. An agency and a labor organization which had been accorded exclusive recognition were required to "meet at reasonable times and confer with respect to personnel policy and practices and matters affecting working conditions, so far as may be appropriate subject to law and policy requirements." Although the scope of bargaining was considerably more restricted than in the private sector, Executive Order 10988 provided a tremendous impetus for organization at the federal level as well as at the state and local level.

On October 29, 1969, President Nixon promulgated Executive Order 11491 which updated and modified Executive Order 10988. It provides for exclusive representational rights only, eliminating informal and formal representation rights. In addition to giving the Assistant Secretary of Labor for Labor-Management Relations the authority to resolve representation matters and to decide unfair labor practice charges and alleged violations of the standards of conduct for labor organizations which are enumerated in the order, Executive Order 10988 establishes a Federal Labor Relations Council to decide policy questions and a Federal Services Impasses Panel to mediate and/or resolve disputes that arise during collective negotiations. While this executive order expands the rights granted labor organizations, the limited scope of negotiations remains essentially the same.

POSTAL REORGANIZATION ACT

Subchapter II of the Postal Reorganization Act of 1970 constitutes a substantial departure in the treatment of postal employees with respect to collective bargaining. Formerly postal employees were covered under Executive Orders 10988 and 11491. They now come under the labor relations provisions of the Postal Reorganization Act which incorporates most of the provisions of the Labor-Management Relations Act (LMRA) and grants jurisdiction to the National Labor Relations Board to resolve representation questions and to decide unfair labor practice allegations. The most important differences between the two laws are that the postal law prohibits strikes, outlaws any form of union security other than the voluntary checkoff of union dues, and requires fact-finding and, if necessary, binding arbitration of collective bargaining impasses.

Since the Postal Reorganization Act provides that unions accorded exclusive recognition have the right to bargain over hours, wages, and other terms and conditions of employment, the scope of bargaining in the Postal Service largely parallels the scope of bargaining in the private sector and is considerably broader than the permissible scope of bargaining under Executive Order 11491. Unlike Executive Order 11491, the Postal Reorganization Act does not contain a statutory management rights provision. To the contrary, there is language in the Postal Reorganization Act which indicates that union proposals seeking to restrict technological changes or to prohibit subcontracting are mandatory subjects of bargaining.

The Postal Reorganization Act will undoubtedly have a tremendous impact on the development of collective bargaining in the federal sector. The *AFL-CIO News* underscored this conclusion when it observed that the postal agreement hammered out in April 1970 by the government and the postal unions and which formed the basis of the labor relations provisions of the Postal Reorganization Act "paves the way for millions of federal workers not only to join a union, but to bargain collectively with their employer on all issues." Although the Postal Service is now an independent establishment within the executive branch of the federal government, the labor relations precedents established by the Postal Service and the unions with which it deals will be looked to by other unions representing federal employees, as well as by unions representing state and local employees.

Because of the different and far more liberal treatment of postal employees under the Postal Reorganization Act, some commentators have declared that Executive Order 11491 is outdated. A report issued by the American Bar Association (ABA) Committee on the Law of Federal Government Employee Relations concluded that the strikes in 1970 by the postal employees and the air traffic controllers made Executive Order 11491 "obsolete." The AFL-CIO has stated that the task ahead is to extend full bargaining rights to all federal government employees and not just postal employees.

That the trend is definitely toward further liberalization of Executive Order 11491 can be gleaned from statements of government administrators responsible for implementing the order. In 1971 both Secretary of Labor James D. Hodgson and Civil Service Commission Chairman Robert E. Hampton viewed Executive Order 11491 as an interim measure that will gradually be revised to allow bargaining on a wider range of subjects. Since the trend seems clear, if not inexorable, that the scope of bargaining will steadily move toward that permitted by the Postal Reorganization Act, the course of collective bargaining in the Postal Service could in large part determine the future course of collective bargaining in the federal sector and also have an influence on state laws.

STATE LEGISLATION

The variety of legislation passed by the various state legislatures in the past decade justifies continued faith in our federal-state form of government and in Justice Holmes' oft-quoted observation that the states constitute "insulated chambers" for "the making of social experiments that an important part of the community desires. . . ." The very variety of the state legislation that has been enacted to date makes the task of analyzing it in detail impossible within the confines of this chapter. It is possible, however, to categorize broadly the state legislation that has been passed and then to discuss how the various state acts treat the following major subjects of concern: (1) right to organize and bargain collectively, (2) determination of appropriate bargaining units, (3) scope of bargaining, (4) resolution of collective bargaining impasses, (5) strike prohibitions, and (6) union security arrangements.

Wisconsin in 1959 was the first state to enact comprehensive legislation concerning collective bargaining for all public employees except those employed by the state. Since then, well over half of the states have enacted legislation covering some or all categories of public employees. The following is a summary of the legislation adopted to date:

Twenty-one states have enacted reasonably comprehensive statutes of general applicability: California (all municipal and state employees; two statutes), Connecticut (all municipal employees), Delaware (all public employees), Hawaii (all public employees), Kansas (all public employees; local option as to coverage), Maine (all municipal employees), Massachusetts (all public employees), Michigan (all public employees except classified state employees), Minnesota (all public employees), Nebraska (all public employees), Nevada (all local government employees), New Hampshire (classified state employees and nonacademic university employees), New Jersey (all public employees), New York (all public employees), Oregon (all state employees and employees of local governments that elect to be covered), Pennsylvania (all public employees), Rhode Island (all state and municipal employees), South Dakota (all public employees), Vermont (all state and municipal employees; two statutes), Washington (all local government employees), and Wisconsin (all state and municipal employees; two statutes).

Fifteen states have enacted separate statutes covering teachers: Alaska, California, Connecticut, Delaware, Idaho, Kansas, Maryland,

Minnesota, Montana, Nebraska, North Dakota, Oregon, Rhode Island, Vermont, and Washington.

Ten states have enacted statutes covering firemen and/or policemen: Alabama (firemen), Florida (firemen), Georgia (firemen), Idaho (firemen), Oklahoma (both), Pennsylvania (both), Rhode Island (both), South Dakota (both), Wyoming (firemen), and Vermont (firemen).

In addition to the foregoing, a number of states have enacted legislation that covers only transit authorities, port authorities, or other special districts. Several states have also enacted legislation covering only health care facilities and/or hospitals.

It seems clear that there will be more legislation enacted at the state level as more states respond affirmatively to the challenge of public employee unionism. This raises the question of whether federal legislation will or should be enacted to govern public employee labor relations at the state and local level. Several bills have already been introduced in Congress that would establish federal hegemony over public sector labor relations. While the Supreme Court has apparently cleared the way insofar as the constitutionality of such legislation is concerned, there is considerable doubt whether any of these bills will be given serious consideration in the foreseeable future. In the first place, the public employee unions that have endorsed federal legislation, recognizing the hard political realities, readily admit that their primary purpose is to goad the states into action. Thus, the model bills that have been submitted as the basis for federal legislation by the American Federation of State, County, and Municipal Employees and the National Education Association have been used by these same organizations as the basis for state legislation. Secondly, the fact that an increasing number of states have enacted legislation reduces the pressure for enactment of legislation by Congress.

One possibility for the enactment of federal legislation, however, should be noted. It has been suggested by some that federal legislation should be enacted to apply only to those states that have not enacted reasonably similar legislation of their own. If a significant minority of states refuse to enact reasonably comprehensive legislation, then pressures could very well build for enactment of federal legislation that would apply to these states.

Meet-and-Confer Approach versus Negotiations Approach

Initially, the state acts can be divided into two categories—those that embody the "meet and confer" approach and those that embody the "negotiations" approach. Implicit in the "meet and confer" approach are the assumptions that the private sector bargaining model is not applicable to the public sector because of the differences between the public and private sectors and that these differences require that public employers retain greater managerial discretion. Thus, under the "meet and confer" approach, as the Advisory Commission on Intergovernmental Relations noted, "the outcome of public employer-employee discussions depends more on management's determinations than on bilateral decisions by 'equals.' " On the other hand, the statutes that embody the "negotiations" approach tend to treat both parties at the bargaining table as equals and contemplate that the decision as to contract terms will be bilateral. Eight states—California, Idaho (teachers), Kansas, Minnesota, Missouri, Montana (teachers), Oregon (teachers), and South Dakota—have enacted "meet and confer" statutes. The remaining state acts, which constitute a clear majority, are negotiation-type statutes. The trend is definitely away from the "meet and confer" approach and toward the "negotiation" approach. In fact, the "meet and confer" approach can and perhaps should be viewed as an interim measure between no collective bargaining and full collective bargaining.

Summary of Major Provisions of State Legislation

Virtually all of the state statutes affirmatively provide that public employees have the right to join and form unions and to bargain collectively. Representative of the provisions found in most of the state statutes is Section 423.209 of the Michigan Public Employment Relations Act:

> It shall be lawful for public employees to organize together or to form, join or assist in labor organizations, to engage in lawful concerted activities for the purpose of collective negotiation or bargaining or other mutual aid and protection, or to negotiate or bargain collectively with their public employers through representatives of their own choosing.

While the comprehensive state statutes generally make it an unfair labor practice for public employers and unions alike to interfere with an employee's right to organize and bargain collectively and establish an administrative agency to implement the unfair labor practice provisions, the separate state acts covering teachers and police and/or fire fighters generally do not have unfair labor practice provisions or establish administrative machinery to implement the rights granted such employees.

DETERMINATION OF APPROPRIATE BARGAINING UNITS

The determination of the appropriate bargaining unit under the comprehensive state acts is made by the agency that administers the act in accordance with criteria set forth in the statute or in rules and regulations promulgated by the administrative agency. The following are the most commonly mentioned criteria:

1. A clear and identifiable community of interest among the employees concerned.
2. The effect of the unit on the efficiency of operations.
3. The history, if any, of employee representation.
4. Supervisory and managerial employees shall not be included in the same unit with nonsupervisory employees.
5. No unit shall include both professional and nonprofessional employees unless a majority of the professional employees vote for inclusion in such a unit.
6. The extent of organization shall not be controlling.

While there is, as indicated, considerable difference in the criteria specified in the various state acts, there is a discernible trend toward criteria that explicitly attempt to avoid the establishment of fragmented bargaining units. For example, the Pennsylvania act provides that in determining the appropriateness of a unit, the board shall "take into consideration but shall not be limited to the following: (i) public employees must have an identifiable community of interest, and (ii) the effects of over-fragmentization." It further provides that the Pennsylvania board shall "take into consideration that when the Commonwealth is the employer, it will be bargaining on a Statewide basis unless the issues involve working conditions peculiar to a given governmental employment locale." Similarly, the Kansas act directs the PERB to consider "the effects of over-fragmentation and the splintering of a work organization."

SCOPE OF BARGAINING

Under the National Labor Relations Act, employers and unions are required to bargain in good faith with respect "to wages, hours and other terms and conditions of employment." Over the years this term of art has been broadly construed to include most matters that affect employees. Many of the state acts use exactly the same language in defining the scope of bargaining between public employers and the employee organizations with which they negotiate. Whether these state acts will receive the same broad interpretation remains to be seen, especially since the circumstances and constraints on bargaining in the public sector may not make the precedents established in the private entirely applicable to the public sector. The big difference may be the role of civil service in the public sector.

Perhaps in recognition of the differences between bargaining in the private sector and bargaining in the public sector, several state acts do not use the same phraseology as the National Labor Relations Act, but rather provide that the parties shall negotiate in good faith "with respect to grievance procedures and conditions of employment." While some have questioned whether this language is broad enough to encompass wages and hours of work, these provisions will in all likelihood be construed to cover such basic items unless specifically exempted. It is nevertheless arguable that the legislatures in question did not intend that the scope of bargaining be as broadly defined as it has been in the private sector.

Although many states broadly define the scope of bargaining, a significant number of them specifically exempt certain subjects from the scope of bargaining. The most prevalent exception concerns civil service systems and the merit principle. For example, Connecticut (for municipal employees), Kansas, and Maine provide that the conduct and grading of merit examinations and the appointment of individuals from lists established by such examinations are not negotiable. The Hawaii, Rhode Island (state employees), Vermont (state employees), Washington, and Wisconsin (state employees) statutes also exempt, in varying degrees, the merit system from the scope of bargaining. Hawaii, for example, provides that the parties "shall not agree to any proposal which would be inconsistent with merit principles."

Following the lead of the federal government in Executive Orders 10988 and 11491, several states have also limited the scope of bargaining by enumerating certain management rights or prerogatives that are retained by public employers. New Hampshire, for example, provides that:

> The State retains the exclusive right through its department heads and appointing authorities, subject to provisions of law and the personal regulations (a) to direct and supervise employees, (b) to appoint, promote, discharge, transfer or demote employees, (c) to lay off unnecessary employees, (d) to maintain the efficiency of government operations, (e) to determine the means, methods and personnel by which operations are to be conducted, and (f) to take whatever actions are necessary to carry out the mission of the agency or department in situations of emergency.

Hawaii, Kansas, Nevada, and Wisconsin (for state employees) have nearly identical provisions.

The serious difficulties which the scope of bargaining poses in the public sector is no better illustrated than in the educational context. On the one hand, the American Federation of Teachers and the National Education Association have asserted that all education policies are the proper subject for negotiation. The National Education Association's "Guidelines for Professional Negotiations" provide that:

> Teachers and other members of the professional staff have an interest in the conditions which attract and retain a superior teaching force in the in-service training programs, in class size, in the selection of textbooks, and in other matters which go far beyond those which would be included in a narrow definition of working conditions. Negotiations should include all matters which affect the quality of the educational system.

School boards, on the other hand, have adamantly insisted that matters pertaining to basic education policy, such as curriculum and textbook selection, should not be negotiable. Dr. Willard R. Lane of the University of Iowa has correctly observed that this problem is considerably more exacerbated in the public sector than in the private sector:

> In the private sector the employer's right to design and control the kind and quality of the product he wishes has been left relatively unchallenged. In education, many of the demands frequently made in negotiations challenge these same professional prerogatives.

Many of the state acts attempt to deal with this admittedly complex problem. Maine, for example, provides "that public employers of teachers shall be required to meet and consult but not negotiate with respect to educational policies." The Montana teacher statute is more specific:

> The matters of negotiation and bargaining for agreement shall not include matters of curriculum, policy of operation, selection of teachers and other personnel, or physical plant of schools or other school facilities, however, nothing herein shall limit the obligation of employers to meet and confer . . . [on these items].

There seems to be a trend, albeit not uniform, toward recognition of the fact that certain educational policies are not appropriately resolved solely through collective bargaining, but rather should be resolved in a broader forum in which various interest groups, including teachers, have a right to participate. The Maine and Montana statutes reflect this trend.

IMPASSE PROCEDURES

Virtually all of the state legislation concerning public employees establishes procedures to resolve collective bargaining disputes. The most prevalent procedure provides for mediation, followed by factfinding with nonbinding recommendations. This is the approach adopted by more than a dozen states, including Connecticut, Michigan, New Jersey, New York, and Wisconsin. While some of the acts set forth the criteria to be used by the fact-finder, most of the acts, such as the New York act, merely provide that the fact-finder is to "make and issue findings of fact and recommendations."

There is also a trend toward encouraging the parties to establish their own impasse procedures, including the use of binding arbitration. Hawaii, for example, provides that "a public employer shall have the power to enter into written agreement with the exclusive representative of an appropriate bargaining unit setting forth an impasse procedure culminating in a final and binding decision, to be invoked in the event of an impasse over the terms of an initial or renewed agreement." Other states that authorize voluntary arbitration of interest disputes include Connecticut, Delaware, Maine, New Jersey, New York, Oregon, Pennsylvania, and Vermont. (Arbitration of interest disputes should be distinguished from arbitration of rights disputes. The former concerns unresolved disputes over what the basic agreement should contain. The latter concerns disputes over the interpretation or application of the collective bargaining agreement.)

Despite the considerable resistance to compulsory arbitration to resolve interest disputes in this country, an increasing number of states have enacted compulsory arbitration statutes, especially for employees who provide essential services such as police and firemen. Four states—Pennsylvania, Michigan, Rhode Island, and South Dakota—provide for compulsory arbitration of interest disputes for both firemen and policemen. Vermont and Wyoming have similar legislation covering only firemen.

Only one state has enacted compulsory arbitration legislation of general applicability. Nevada recently amended its public employee bargaining statute to give the governor the authority to direct, prior to the submission of the dispute to fact-finding, that the findings and recommendations on some or all issues be final and binding. Two other states—Maine and Rhode Island—have statutes that provide for compulsory arbitration of some but not all negotiable issues if the parties are unable to reach agreement. Maine provides that the arbitrator's decision is binding "with respect to a controversy over subjects other than salaries, pensions and insurance." The Rhode Island statute for municipal employees calls for binding arbitration "on all matters not involving the expenditure of money."

Although there is a trend toward the enactment of more statutes calling for compulsory arbitration, it is difficult to say that this trend will continue in the future. Indeed, it appears that considerable opposition is mounting in many states to compulsory arbitration. There has been, for example, considerable opposition in Michigan to the compulsory arbitration statute for police and firemen. That statute was enacted on an experimental basis for a period of only two years, and it remains to be seen whether it will be reenacted.

Finally, it should be noted that the various impasse procedures set forth in the state acts are generally tied to the budget process. For example, the timetable for mediation and fact-finding is usually related to the budget submission date. The budget process and the availability of funds also have considerable practical implications insofar as the scope of bargaining is concerned.

STRIKE PROHIBITIONS

As previously noted, strikes by public employees are uniformly considered to be illegal at common law. Not surprisingly, an overwhelming number of the state acts expressly prohibit strikes by all public employees. There is a wide variety of remedies, however. In some states, such as Rhode Island, Washington, and Delaware, strikes are merely declared illegal, leaving it to the public employer to seek an injunction, take disciplinary action, or pursue whatever other remedies may be available. In several other states, including Kansas, Massachusetts, and Wisconsin, strikes are deemed to be unfair labor practices and thus subject to cease and desist orders issued by the agency responsible for administering the act. The Kansas statute provides, however, that a public employer is authorized to seek injunctive relief while such unfair labor practice proceedings are pending before the Kansas board.

In a few states the remedies and/or procedures to be followed in the event of a strike are spelled out in considerable detail. For example, the New York Taylor Act provides that if a union appears to have violated the strike prohibitions set forth in the statute, the chief legal officer of the public employer is required to "apply to the Supreme Court for an injunction against such violation." The Taylor Act, like several other acts, also sets forth certain sanctions for violation of the no-strike prohibition. Thus, any public employee who violates the prohibition against strikes is placed on probation for one year and the public employer is directed to "deduct from the compensation of each such public employee an amount equal to twice his daily rate of pay for each day or part thereof that it was determined that he had violated this subdivision." The New York law further provides that any public employee who violates the no-strike prohibition "may be subject to removal or other disciplinary action provided by law for misconduct." In addition to sanctions against individuals, the Taylor Act sets forth certain sanctions and penalties that can be imposed against any employee organization that violates the no-strike provisions of the act. Thus, the act provides that such an employee organization forfeits its right to have the dues of its members checked off for a period of time to be determined by the PERB. The act further provides that an employee organization that "willfully disobeys a lawful mandate of a court of record, or wilfully offers resistance to such lawful mandate, in a case involving or growing out of [an illegal] strike . . . ," may be fined for each day that such contempt continues in an amount "fixed in the discretion of the Court."

The Hawaii, Pennsylvania, and Vermont acts stand in sharp contrast to the other state acts in that they permit strikes by some categories of public employees.[1] The Vermont act covering municipal employees provides that "no public employee may strike or recognize a picket

---

[1] Montana also has a statute covering nurses employed by both public and private health care facilities which allows nurses to strike if thirty days notice has been given and if there is not "another strike in effect at another health care facility within a radius of 150 miles."

line of a labor organization while performing his official duties, if the strike or recognition of a picket line will endanger the health, safety or welfare of the public." The act then authorizes a public employer to seek injunctive relief in the event such a strike or recognition of a picket line occurs or is about to occur. Since all public employee strikes will not presumably "endanger the health, safety or welfare of the public," the Vermont legislation implicitly permits some categories of municipal employees to strike. The decision as to whether a given strike endangers the health, safety, or welfare will be made by the court on a case-by-case basis.

Both the Hawaii and Pennsylvania acts explicitly permit some categories of public employees to strike, but only after the statutory impasse procedures have been exhausted. Hawaii thus conditions the right to strike upon (1) a good faith compliance with the statutory impasse procedures, including exhaustion of any unfair labor practice proceeding, (2) the passage of 60 days from the time the findings and recommendations of a fact-finding board are made public, and (3) the giving of a 10-day notice of intent to strike to the public employee relations board and the employer by the union. While all categories of public employees are covered by this provision, the act further provides that:

> Where the strike occurring, or about to occur, endangers the public health or safety, the public employer concerned may petition the board to make an investigation. If the board finds that there is imminent a present danger to the health and safety of the public, the board shall set requirements that must be complied with to avoid or remove any such imminent or present danger.

The Pennsylvania act specifically prohibits strikes by guards at mental hospitals or prisons and personnel necessary to the functioning of the courts. (Policemen and firemen are covered by a separate act that provides for compulsory arbitration and prohibits strikes.) Strikes by all other categories of public employees, if the mediation and fact-finding procedures "have been completely utilized and exhausted," are permissible:

> . . . unless or until such a strike creates a clear and present danger or threat to the health, safety or welfare of the public. In such cases the public employer shall initiate, in the court of common pleas of the jurisdiction where such strike occurs, an action for equitable relief including but not limited to appropriate injunctions and shall be entitled to such relief if the court finds that the strike creates a clear and present danger to the health, safety or welfare of the public.

The Hawaii and Pennsylvania acts undoubtedly represent a trend away from the absolute prohibition of all public employee strikes.

Whether the Hawaii and Pennsylvania acts are broadly representative of a nationwide trend, or merely representative of the political realities in those two states, remains to be seen. Perhaps equally representative is the action of the New York State Legislature in 1969 in strengthening—not weakening—the anti-strike provisions of the Taylor Act. We also note that, while some state advisory groups have recommended that strikes by nonessential employees should be permitted in some circumstances, the Advisory Commission on Intergovernmental Relations unequivocally stated that "compelling reasons exist for prohibiting any public employees from engaging in strikes." In short, this whole area is in a state of transition. Hopefully, the experience under the divergent legislative schemes governing public sector strikes will prove helpful in assessing their strengths and weaknesses.

UNION SECURITY ARRANGEMENTS

Most of the state acts provide that public employees have the right to join or refrain from joining a union. As a result, union security provisions that would require an employee to belong to a union (union shop), to maintain membership in a union (maintenance of membership), or to pay union dues or a service fee equivalent to such dues to a union (agency shop) as a condition of employment are generally not permitted. There are two major exceptions to this otherwise uniform prohibition of these union security arrangements. Hawaii requires an employer, upon receipt of a written statement from a union having exclusive bargaining rights specifying the "reasonable service fees necessary to defray the costs for its services rendered in negotiating and administering an agreement and computed on a prorated basis among all employees," to deduct "from every employee in the appropriate unit" the service fee thus specified and to remit the amount collected to the union. Pennsylvania provides that maintenance of membership is a "proper subject of bargaining," but further specifies that "the payment of dues and assessments while members, may be the only requisite employment condition."

Judicial interpretation of the Michigan act should also be noted. The Michigan Employment Relations Commission ruled in a split decision that, while the union shop is illegal, the agency shop under which nonmembers would be required as a condition of employment to pay an amount equal to the union's regular dues was legal (*Oakland County Sheriff's Dept.*, 1968). The Michigan Court of Appeals, however, added a further requirement in *Smigel v. Southgate Community School District* (1970). It held that the validity of an agency shop clause "hinges on the relationship between payment of a sum equivalent to the dues of . . . [the union] and a nonmember's proportionate share of the cost of negotiating and administering the contract involved." The court further held that if the "payment is greater than or less than the proportionate share, the agency shop provision is in violation of" the Michigan Public Employment Relations Act.

While the voluntary deduction of union dues is not, technically speaking, a form of union security, it is usually discussed along with union security arrangements since it does contribute substantially to the financial security and strength of the union. The voluntary checkoff of union dues is expressly authorized under many of the state acts. And in many of the states where it is not expressly authorized in the public employee labor relations act, it is authorized by previously enacted legislation or applicable court decisions.

Conclusion

Collective bargaining in the public sector is in many respects at the same state of development as collective bargaining was in the private sector in the late 1930s. Like the private sector then, the public sector is beset with militancy and there is considerable uncertainty as to what the future holds. Some of the same dour warnings about the evils of collective bargaining that were heard in the private sector following passage of the Wagner Act in 1935 are being heard today about bargaining in the public sector. But, as the National Governors' Conference *Report of Task Force on State and Local Government Labor Relations* noted, "Neither the pillars of city halls nor the foundations of the civil service crumbled when conditions of employment were negotiated instead of being fixed unilaterally." While much remains to be resolved, it is not unreasonable to suggest that, as precedents are established to govern the conduct of the parties and as the parameters of bargaining become more firmly established, the degree of militancy present today will decrease. That, at least, was the experience in the private sector. We are not suggesting that the problems are easy or that everything will eventually work out satisfactorily for all concerned. We do suggest, as the parties become more experienced in their relatively new roles and as institutional changes are made to accommodate to the reality of collective bargaining, the crisis, conflict, and confrontation that permeates much of public sector bargaining will begin to recede.

Arvid Anderson

3

The Structure of Public Sector Bargaining

Who Bargains for What, with Whom, and Why?

The question of who bargains for what, with whom, and why is not merely of academic or legal interest. We have learned that the answers to the questions regarding the composition of the bargaining unit, the scope of bargaining, the authority to bargain for the employer, and the legal rules for playing the game often predetermine the results of bargaining.

The structure of public sector bargaining has grown both *de jure* and *de facto*. Statutes have been enacted at the local, state, and federal levels in various jurisdictions permitting or protecting and encouraging the right to bargain collectively. Other laws have been passed which are solely negative, prohibiting strikes by public employees, but providing no affirmative protection for the right to organize and bargain collectively.

The federal courts have extended constitutional guarantees to protect the right to organize in those jurisdictions where state statutes have not conferred or attempted to prohibit such right. In other jurisdictions, in the absence of state legislation, executive orders issued by governors, mayors, or county executives have established bargaining rights for public employees. In still other jurisdictions the attorney general, corporation counsel, or city attorney has rendered opinions affirming some form of organizational rights or collective bargaining procedures for public employees.

In a number of other jurisdictions, state statutes have permitted employees to meet-and-confer rather than bargain with public employ-

ARVID ANDERSON *is chairman of the New York City Office of Collective Bargaining and is a former commissioner of the Wisconsin Employment Relations Board. He has been a mediator, arbitrator, and university lecturer.*

ees. In some cities, Chicago for example, in the absence of a statute bargaining takes place on a *de facto* basis with those unions powerful enough to insist on bargaining, such as teachers, policemen and firemen. Thus, the past decade has been marked by a rapid increase in the number of states enacting laws to conduct employment relations with their public employees. But bargaining has not been stopped in the absence of such laws. The absence of laws has only meant that bargaining has not been regulated and that unions or employers who need the protection of bargaining laws do without. The record of strike activity as reported by the Bureau of Labor Statistics shows almost as many strikes in states without bargaining laws as have occurred in heavily organized states with such laws.

What the absence of laws does mean is the absence of procedures for dealing with questions of representation, arbitrability of grievances, scope of bargaining, unfair or improper labor practices. Strikes for recognition are the second largest cause of public sector disputes, but are now virtually unknown in the private sector where state and federal laws provide procedures for resolving representation disputes.

The absence of laws has also meant the creation of a patchwork bargaining structure comprised of units that have sprung into being without benefit of guidelines or criteria, inevitably leading to endless bargaining problems.

The laws which have been enacted have been described in chapter 2 and are of a considerable variety. Some statutes are comprehensive and apply to all public employees in the jurisdiction while others are limited to special categories of employees such as nurses, fire fighters, teachers, policemen, municipal transit and utility workers. Bargaining statutes have been established in Los Angeles County for municipal transit and utility employees for the reason that such employees formerly enjoyed the protection of private sector bargaining laws, state and federal, when they were employed by a private corporation and then when the utility was converted to a public corporation bargaining rights for the transit employees were continued under a public statute. Parallel experiences exist in other jurisdictions where privately owned transit and utility services have been taken over by public authorities.

In some states, New York and Wisconsin for example, prevailing wage statutes are applicable to some skilled tradesmen employed by governments. Their pay is actually determined by private sector bargaining. Postal workers have a separate bargaining statute based on the private sector law, the Taft-Hartley Law, while other federal workers have bargaining rights, fixed under the terms of Executive Order 11491. The majority of the statutes which have been enacted and the bargaining practices which have evolved in the private sector have followed a private sector pattern with some modifications for the public sector, particularly on the restriction or prohibition of the strike. Examples of private sector labor relations statutes transferred to the public sector are the Wisconsin statute for municipal employees enacted in 1962, the Michigan statute for municipal employees of 1965, and the Postal Reorganization Law of 1970 which brought postal labor relations under some of the provisions of the Labor-Management Relations Act.

Bargaining Units and Criteria

The "who" of who bargains is strongly conditioned by the limitations of the bargaining unit. Establishment of an overall bargaining unit tends to smother the interests peculiar to professionals or skilled employees. On the other hand the establishment of multifragmented units causes many bargaining problems.

During the early growth of public employee bargaining, unit problems did not receive the attention which they have subsequently been given. Bargaining units were established, for example, in New York City and under the Federal Executive Order 10988 on a building block theory—informal, formal, and exclusive. Unions which represented less than 10 percent of the employees of a proposed bargaining unit were granted informal recognition. Unions with more than 10 percent but less than 50 percent of representation in a bargaining unit were granted formal recognition. Exclusive recognition was granted to majority representatives in an appropriate bargaining unit. The purpose of the building block approach was to encourage employee organization as a step to full-scale collective bargaining. In practice this meant units were established with varying degrees of bargaining rights on the basis of extent of union organization by job title and by department. As the scope of bargaining was limited under the building block approach in New York City and under Executive Order 10988, there was little concern about the long-range consequences of a large number of small bargaining units. However, with the advent of full-scale collective bargaining in New York City, meaning bargaining over wages, hours and working conditions, the problem of determining appropriate units became acute.

Units which were suitable for building block organizational purposes created enormous interunion rivalries when bargaining on wages, hours, and conditions of employment was mandated. Unions representing essentially the same job titles in different departments tried to outdo each other in bargaining. For example, locals of the Service Employees International Union, the Teamsters, and the American Federation of State, County and Municipal Employees (AFSCME) all represented similar clerical and maintenance titles in New York City.

Highly fragmented bargaining units, in which the same category of occupational titles is represented by different unions, also have resulted in chain reactions and unduly delayed bargaining. For example, superior officers of the police and fire departments of New York City delay bargaining until a contract is settled for the line organizations. Smaller units and unions assume a dog-in-the-manger posture either by choice or because the employer prefers to settle with a larger union or a different pacesetter. The principal issues in a highly fragmented bargaining structure are "me-too" and one upmanship.

One of the solutions to fragmentation has been to encourage coordinated bargaining by employees generally in the same or related pay grades or occupational groups. Sometimes such coordination has been compelled by legislation which imposes upon the employer the duty to bargain only with a union which represents a majority of the employees in similar occupational groups or categories. An example of this is the bargaining on a citywide basis for pensions referred to earlier.

In some jurisdictions labor relations agencies have been able to consolidate impasse panel proceedings involving similar or related bargaining groups such as police and fire. For example, in New York City a three-member impasse panel considered the issues in the police, fire, and sanitation disputes making a joint report that included similar recommendations for each service. Like procedures can be effective when dealing with complicated and difficult issues such as whether policemen and firemen should receive the same pay. But the solution most likely to avoid fragmentation is a conscious policy of the labor relations agency to create the optimum number of bargaining units in its jurisdiction.

Bargaining unit criteria vary from state to state, but are usually based upon familar private sector standards, such as the community of interest and the wishes of the employees. Some public sector statutes recognize that in addition to the foregoing the factors of the authority of the employer to bargain and sound labor relations must also be considered in establishing appropriate bargaining units.

Moreover, the question of the authority of the employer to bargain is a much more complex and important question in government than in the industrial sector, where normally a fixed authority with responsibility for bargaining easily can be established. This is seldom true in the public service because of the separation of powers—executive, legislative, judicial. Special public authorities, such as transit, utility, and bistate bridge and port authorities pose special problems in terms of bargaining laws and the authority to bargain.

Who determines the bargaining unit is also an important question. Under state statutes this responsibility may have been given to a labor relations agency, such as the New York State Public Employment Relations Board, the Board of Certification of the Office of Collective Bargaining in New York City, the Michigan Labor Relations Commission, the Wisconsin Employment Relations Commission, or any one of the number of state agencies. In the case of the federal government, the National Labor Relations Board has the responsibility for determining units in the Postal Service and the Assistant Secretary of Labor for employees covered by Executive Order 11491. The labor relations agency determines the appropriate unit, procedures for the conduct of elections, and the time during which representation questions properly may be raised. The determination of the appropriate bargaining unit is not merely a ministerial act, but determines in large part the structure of bargaining.

In the absence of a statutory procedure for determining appropriate units a bargaining unit may have been established by voluntary recognition by the public employer; or the statute may authorize the public employer initially to recognize voluntarily a unit if he is satisfied that an employee organization represents a majority of the employees involved. Bargaining units in some cases have been established by legislation, which was done in the State of Hawaii and by the federal government in Canada. Statutes usually provide procedures for reviewing the unit determinations of labor relations agencies in this matter.

To a public employer, establishing the most appropriate bargaining unit usually means a broad occupational unit representing employees in skilled, professional, or technical occupations; craft, blue collar, or white collar employees; and uniformed or law enforcement groups.

Typical exclusions from bargaining units have been managerial, executive, and confidential employees. Managerial and executive employees have been defined as employees who either make or implement policy, including labor relations policy, or who effectively recommend important actions with respect to personnel in such matters as promotion, transfer, discipline, pay increases, and the like.

But even with standards, determining in fact who are managerial, executive, or confidential employees in terms of labor relations or policy making and implementation has been and continues to be a complicated task for labor relations agencies. If employees are excluded from bargaining units because their inclusion would constitute a conflict of interest the question arises as to what procedures for alternative benefits have been provided by the employer for the excluded employees. Some public employers have established a policy of giving excluded employees at least as many benefits as they would have received from collective bargaining. Examples of such procedures are the managerial and executive pay plans which have been developed in New York City and under the federal executive order.

Special problems exist with respect to *supervisory units*. Should supervisors have the right to bargain? If so, should they be in unions or units separate from nonsupervisory employees? The problem of who is a supervisory employee is complex. Job titles in government routinely include the term supervisor for all but the entry job in an occupational series even though the actual job may require little or no supervision. For example, a secretarial series may have five or six levels; all but the entry title will include supervision in the job description. In practice the supervisory title may really be a means of compensating an employee for experience, responsibility and skills, but not actual supervision.

Appropriate unit determinations are related to different subject matters of bargaining. New York City, because of the great multiplicity of bargaining units which were created prior to the enactment of the New York City Collective Bargaining Law in 1967, established by that law different levels of bargaining to deal with different subject matters of bargaining. For example, only a union which represents a majority of all employees in the career and salary plan may negotiate on conditions which must be uniform for all employees in the plan, such as time and leave rules and pensions. "Career and salary employees" includes virtually all civil service employees except the uniformed forces and the skilled trades. Time and leave rules are defined to include such subjects as overtime, sick leave, vacations, holiday pay, and the like.

In New York City individually certified unions negotiate on wage rates for the citywide occupational titles which they represent, such as internes and residents. But a union which has been *designated* as a majority representative for *all* career and salary occupational titles may negotiate a citywide agreement covering benefits that must be uniform, including pensions. The different levels of bargaining also relate to the authority of the representative employer. Delineations of levels of bargaining have brought some problems between unions. Charges of violation of Article XX of the AFL-CIO No-Raiding Agreement have stemmed from the different levels of bargaining in New York City. Several cases are now under review.

EXCLUSIVE REPRESENTATION

The majority of laws which have established collective bargaining rights have established the right of the majority representative to be designated or certified as the *exclusive representative* who also has the right to negotiate for or to receive the exclusive dues checkoff. The lack of certification or designation as the exclusive bargaining representative leads to a continuing rivalry and battling for majority status.

WHO BARGAINS FOR THE PUBLIC EMPLOYER?

W. Willard Wirtz when secretary of labor emphasized the need for governmental employers at the bargaining table to be able to say "I will or I won't" rather than "I can't." Obviously Mr. Wirtz referred to the necessity of governmental representatives to make effective recommendations or decisions on behalf of their principals.

[The separation of powers in government between the executive and legislative branches is one of the basic distinctions between the governmental employer and the private sector employer.] However, despite the problems effective public service bargaining requires that the authority of the governmental employer to bargain be fixed insofar as is possible. [Public employment bargaining authority may be vested by law in the executive or the legislature or a combination thereof.]

The Connecticut Municipal Statute makes bargaining an executive function with the legislative body being mandated to act upon the contracts negotiated by the executive. In the State of New York and the City of New York bargaining responsibility has been fixed as an executive function. For most districts throughout the country, bargaining is the responsibility of the school board and may be carried on, in fact, by either the superintendent of schools or his representatives. In other jurisdictions actual bargaining is done by members of the school board.

The Wisconsin State Legislature has fixed the employers' bargaining responsibility for state employees in the executive; but in practice the Joint Committee on Finance of the legislature has played a significant role in the bargaining process by maintaining very close liaison with the excutive office bargainers and influencing the terms of the settlement.

A legislative committee of the City Council in Milwaukee has the responsibility for employer bargaining. The bargaining team is employed by and reports to the council committee on personnel and finance. In New York City a labor policy committee has been established to advise and guide the director of the Office of Labor Relations in bargaining with municipal employees. Two deputy mayors, a budget director, personnel director, corporation counsel, and labor relations director serve as the mayor's labor relations policymaking team. Such coordination focuses responsibility on the executive and lessens the possibility of end runs by union representatives to other governmental authority.

The authority of the employer's bargaining team, however constituted, may also be affected by other statutes. For example, the education law, civil service law, welfare laws, statutes affecting police and fire, prevailing wage statutes, pension statutes, statutes affecting the fiscal authority of the municipal employer and the timetable for budget-making, all affect and may operate as constraints on the authority of the public employer. Civil service statutes regulate the method of examination, appointment, promotion, and layoff. Furthermore, the ability of the employer to negotiate certain conditions of seniority and establishing procedures in disciplinary actions are affected by civil service statutes and regulations

State statutes in some jurisdictions regulate the hours of work of policemen or firemen and their tours of duty. Federal and state welfare laws mandate certain costs and standards on the local public employer. Education laws may mandate certain conditions for teacher employment, such as standards of hire, methods of selecting or removing teachers, methods of promotion, or of tenure and the school calendar. In addition, the Fair Labor Standards Act has been extended to public schools and hospitals, thus mandating certain public employment conditions by the federal government on state and local governments.

Pension laws enacted by the state legislature may exclude pensions from bargaining or require legislative approval of changes in pension laws, as in New York State. A major crisis arose and to some extent continues in New York City as a result of the refusal of the 1971 New York Legislature to approve a pension program negotiated by the city and the citywide union bargaining representative. The New York State Legislature declined to vote on the pension proposal although state law mandates that state legislative approval is required before such pension plans can be effective.

The dilution by statutes and the resulting uncertainty of the public employer's bargaining authority in some areas has been a factor in perpetuating the practice of double-deck bargaining or the legislative end run. This technique allows employee organizations to seek improvements upon or obtain benefits from the appropriate legislative body which they were unable to obtain at the bargaining table or which they are required by law to obtain at the legislative level.

The efforts of some legislative bodies to participate directly in bargaining while others stand at arms-length from the process also represent persisting problems affecting the authority to bargain. Unless a working relationship between the bargaining authority and the appropriate legislative body is developed, the legislative end-run and double-deck procedures referred to above will will be encouraged. There is no single answer to this question because problems vary with different jurisdictions, with different charters, and with different experiences.

The problem of the bargaining authority of separately elected executives or officials sometimes arises in the case of sheriffs and county clerks or county executives and the county's legislative body.

The Labor Relations Office—The complexities and demands of labor relations in public employment today require much more than the fixing and definition of the bargaining authority. For one, the public employer should establish an office with a person or persons responsible for the conduct of labor relations. The size of the office and scope of the functions will vary with the size of the jurisdiction, the number of unions, and the scope of the laws governing the bargaining process. The primary function of the labor relations office under whatever title is the representation of the public employer in the negotiation and administration of labor agreements. The office also must represent the public employer in appearances before labor relations agencies in representation proceedings and improper practice procedures, and must be prepared to present the employer's side before arbitrators, impasse panel members, and fact-finders. The office will oversee settlement efforts in grievance cases prior to arbitration and must be familiar with the mediation process. In addition, the labor relations office will need the assistance of legal counsel and a research staff with a knowledge of civil service rules, regulations, job titles, and pay plans to prepare for bargaining and third-party proceedings.

Legal Officer's Role—What is the legal officer's role in coordinating the bargaining or the determination of the labor relations policy of the various department heads and agencies of the city, county, or state government? Is this done by the employment relations officer or the labor relations officer or by the legal officer? The answers to some of the questions as to the role of the legal officer vary depending on whether the subject matter is legal, fiscal, personnel, or political.

The role of the governmental attorney in bargaining is of interest. Is the attorney a part of the employer's bargaining team? Often he is, but if he is an elected or appointed official, which may be the case with a city attorney or an attorney general, it may make some difference as to whether the attorney is of the same political party or persuasion as the executive. Does the governmental attorney represent the labor relations agency, if one exists? Or does such labor relations agency have independent counsel? Because governmental labor relations assumes that the government's role is that of the employer, it necessarily follows that the government is a party to virtually every proceeding before a labor relations agency. Thus, the government lawyer's role must be that of employer. Laws have been enacted in New York State and New York City empowering the labor relations agencies—the state Public Employment Relations Board and the New York City Office of Collective Bargaining—to employ independent counsel.

Training—The public employer requires the skills and services performed by management in the private sector, in addition to the special knowledge and training required to resolve disputes in the public service. The need for training labor relations officers at all levels of government, and the necessity of familiarizing governmental managers with labor relations problems have been recognized. Municipal employers have formed such organizations as the Labor-Management Relations Service, a combination of cities and counties, one of whose functions is to train and appraise municipal officials of collective bargaining developments. Training functions have been undertaken also by the federal government through the United States Civil Service Commission. The Public Personnel Association and the Educators Negotiating Service, private agencies, and various universities have sponsored numerous seminars and training programs for public administrators in public sector labor relations.

COMMUNITY GROUPS

Related to the question of the authority of the bargainer in the public sector is the desire of various community groups to participate in labor relations policy matters, particularly at the local level. These groups range from the Citizens Taxpayer Alliance, League of Women Voters, and parent-teacher associations to new community action groups concerned with problems of poverty, racial minorities, housing, and school problems. Collective bargaining is structured on a bilateral, employer-employee relationship with a focused authority representing the employees and the employer. However the governmental entity, though acting only as an employer, has a broader responsibility to all citizens. Governmental officials find it difficult to exclude political, citizen, or community groups from any role in the bargaining process. While no special rule of procedure is available for the intervention of community action groups in the bargaining process, clearly their views as well as those of the press have an impact on the bargaining.

Scope of Bargaining

When a bargaining authority has been established for the public employer and an employee organization representative has been chosen, the question arises as to the subject matter of bargaining, i.e., what is or is not bargainable. Typically, collective bargaining means wages, hours, and conditions of employment in both public and private employment. But defining such subjects in particular public employment jurisdictions is another matter. Some jurisdictions, by law, limit bargaining while others are wide open.

Collective bargaining in the public service has been described as the process of who gets how much and when. Bargaining is largely over economic items, but by no means exclusively so—and this is particularly true in public employment. Broad categories of bargainable subjects have been established in the public service which are identical to those in the private sector, namely subjects that are mandatory or required, permissive or voluntary, and prohibited. How these various categories of bargaining are determined and by whom is a structural problem of bargaining.

Mandatory subjects would include wages, hours, and fringe benefits such as pensions, health and hospital insurance, vacations, sick leaves, holiday, overtime, and similar benefits. Voluntary or permissive subjects might include joint employer-union recommendations to amend or change civil service or education laws, and promotional opportunities or other personnel changes which by law are within the sole discretion of the employer. Prohibited subjects could include a members-only contract providing benefits only for members of the union where the union had the duty to bargain for all employees. A union shop would be another example in those jurisdictions where a union shop is expressly barred by statute.

Related to the scope of bargaining and the determination of its propriety is the question of what subject matters may properly be submitted to the grievance arbitration process.

RESOLUTION OF SCOPE OF BARGAINING QUESTIONS

How are conflicts over bargaining subjects resolved, given existing collective bargaining, civil service, education, welfare, police and fire statutes, and fiscal constraints? In New York City the Board of Collective Bargaining has the statutory responsibility to make final determinations of disputes as to whether a matter is within the scope of bargaining and thus, in turn, subject to impasse resolution. The New York City experience is particularly significant because it provides for the resolution of disputes over the scope of bargaining, not via the unfair labor practice route of the industrial sector, but by a good faith procedure over bargainability.

There seems little reason to charge an employer with bad faith if he refuses to bargain over certain subjects which he doubts in good faith are bargainable under the statute. For example, a dispute as to whether the school curriculum is bargainable could be submitted to a labor board or court as a good faith dispute rather than via the unfair labor practice route with all the connotations of anti-union animus that such charges bring.

The Board of Collective Bargaining has ruled, for example, on a dispute over whether the number of men in the fire department is a bargainable subject. The board held that the question of workload or manning could become a subject of bargaining or for impasse resolution if there were a demonstration of practical impact. *Practical impact* was defined as a manning table and workload that resulted in unreasonable and excessively burdensome workloads as a regular and continuing condition of employment. In a three-and-one-half-year period the board has issued a number of bargainability rulings including one that a demand to establish the level of benefits for relief recipients was not a required subject of bargaining. The board has pending for determination a dispute as to whether a demand to bargain for a welfare plan on behalf of persons already retired is within the scope of bargaining.

A similar procedure is used in New York City for resolving disputes covering the arbitrability of certain grievances. Objections to arbitrability on substantive, not procedural, grounds are resolved by the Board of Collective Bargaining, which has adopted, in general, the private sector guidelines for resolution of arbitrability questions.

The state Public Employment Relations Board has ruled that layoffs caused by budgetary limitations are not a mandatory subject of bargaining under the Taylor Law, but that the impact of such decision to lay off employees is bargainable.

In some states disputes over the scope of bargaining are resolved on an *ad hoc* basis by impasse panels or by court decisions. Under the terms of Executive Order 11491 disputes over the scope of bargaining are resolved by the Federal Labor Relations Council. Under the Postal Reorganization Act disputes over the scope of bargaining may be resolved through the unfair labor practice sections of the National Labor Relations Act.

A survey of the scope of bargaining questions in New York State schools indicates their range. Teachers have negotiated for and obtained contract provisions covering class size, school days, assignment procedures, school calendar, evaluation procedures, use of school facilities, curriculum planning, lawsuit protection, organization convention attendance, length of class periods, textbook selections, teacher load, policies and practices, and teaching methods. At the same time school administrators have obtained management rights clauses as well as specific reference to operating within education laws and have established procedures and mechanisms for discussing items outside the scope of bargaining. School managements have also succeeded in excluding certain subjects from the grievance procedure. Thus collective bargaining in practice in some New York jurisdictions has attempted a balance as to employee desires and educational needs for school administrators and professional employees.

The determination of scope of bargaining questions is also important because the collective bargaining process itself has been the instrument for creating new structures of dispute resolution and for resolving certain public policy questions. The collective bargaining process established not only new conditions of employment in terms of economic benefits for the postal services, but, in fact, a whole new procedure of bargaining as well as providing the impetus for the new postal corporation.

A basic question remains regarding the extent to which it is appropriate, and in the public interest, for major public policy questions, which extend beyond the scope of the employee-employer relationship, to be determined solely by collective bargaining. For example, should the level of benefits of welfare recipients or the question of school desegregation be determined primarily by collective bargaining? Or, are such issues really the primary responsibility of the executive and legislative function with the employer and employees affected having a voice, but not being the sole determinants in deciding such policy questions?

Timetable for Bargaining

Local, state, and federal statutes may affect the length of the contract and the timetable for bargaining. Budget deadlines, contract deadlines, the commencement of the school year, and previous patterns of bargaining in the public and private sector affect the collective bargaining timetable and the structure for bargaining. Budget deadlines have a varied impact on bargaining. At times these deadlines have been more honored in the breach than in the observance. Bargaining really does not stop in countless jurisdictions because a budget deadline has passed. Numerous governments enact supplemental budgets after negotiations. New York City has been specifically exempted from the budget deadline provisions of the Taylor Law in New York. However, the absence of a legal right to strike and in some instances the lack of an effective strike threat or the absence of alternative dispute settlement machinery make it difficult to bring bargaining to a head. Thus in some jurisdictions the budget deadline may push bargaining to completion. However, it should not serve as a controlling factor in all jurisdictions.

Multi-Employers

The fact of dual public employers in some governmental functions causes structural problems in bargaining. Even if not dual employers, in fact, the joint responsibility of different government levels for the governmental function complicates bargaining. The sheriff may have a dual statutory responsibility with the county executive for his employees. Education is both a state and local responsibility with the federal government also expected to assume a substantial role in meeting education costs—of which personnel is always the largest factor. Thus, in order to carry out a local collective bargaining agreement affecting federal or state programs for highways, health services or education, the *de facto* approval of state and local governments may be required to implement a local government's agreement. That is particularly true of fiscally dependent school districts that depend entirely upon the taxing authority of another unit of government as in the case of the six largest cities of New York State.

Another aspect of the bargaining authority problem for school districts is the necessity in the majority of school districts for taxpayer approval of budgets and in effect the approval of collective bargaining agreements. The large number of rejections of school budgets and local bond issues, while by no means the sole cause, is related to the cost of collective bargaining. The various constraints which exist particularly on local units of government are evidenced by the resistance to property tax increases. Local governments must obtain their taxing authority from the state government which is often reluctant to grant necessary taxing authority to carry out contractual obligations. There is the political as well as the legal question of the ability of the government to pay the benefits which have been negotiated at the collective bargaining table.

Priorities have to be considered by budget makers and administrators. A substantial increase for police and fire services or teachers or unions, whether arrived at by negotiation, arbitration or impasse procedures, may require delays in expenditures for capital construction, schools, and hospitals or may require the layoff of persons performing less essential services. Park employees, particularly seasonal employees, or school aides may have to be laid off in order to retain or pay higher salaries and fringe benefits. The City of Cleveland in 1971 was required to lay off some policemen because of the rejection by the citizens of proposed tax outlays. Such actions require managerial decisions and may induce certain efficiencies and economies in some services, but such actions also involve political decisions. The refusal of the legislature to implement the New York City pension plan referred to above was accompanied by a New York legislative decision to establish a new State Pension Commission to review the costs and procedures for pensions for employees of the state and its political subdivisions.

Criteria for Bargaining

The bargaining structure with respect to grievances and impasses must be flexible enough in order to deal with varying economic conditions and the changing and increasing demand for public services. Collective bargaining during a recession requires a municipal employer and union to give special consideration to questions of manpower utilization and productivity. In those circumstances where reductions in force are effectuated, governmental employers tend to favor attrition as a means of handling cutbacks. Such a device is counterproductive when applied to those services which are either understaffed to begin with, or by the nature of the work performed, associated with a very high turnover. For example, nurses and nurses' aides have a historically high rate of turnover because the services depend heavily on part-time employees. Hospitals cannot be efficiently run if they are not allowed to fill vacancies, or at least a high percentage of the vacancies, that occur. Park services can be curtailed by laying off people, but you cannot maintain an efficient hospital by laying off a large part of the work force. Thus, absent selectivity, attrition can become self-defeating, creating more costly problems than it solves.

Measures of productivity in the conventional sense, such as output per manhour, are only partially applicable to the public service. While the number of licenses issued or tons of garbage collected are integral factors in any consideration of productivity, the factors needed to measure the adequacy of fire and police protection are not so tangible. The greatest number of fires and crimes occur in the late afternoon and evening hours. Thus, scheduling the hours of work and assigning areas of responsibility to policemen and firemen to match variations in demand geographically and by time of day are examples of the most effective application and allocation of manpower.

Modern management techniques such as computer systems can be employed effectively in the public service, but such techniques alone cannot measure the effective delivery and quality of health, education, and welfare services. Unions representing professionals in the health, education, and welfare occupations are demanding the right to bargain over the level and quality of services provided. Bargaining over class size and educational programs raises the question of mutual accountability for the quality of the educational program, but such concepts involve areas traditionally considered to be the exclusive province of management. Thus some management demands for efficient public service will lead to greater participation by employee organizations in making joint determinations of public programs and policies.

Collective bargaining laws and practices have established certain criteria for bargaining. Comparability pay statutes, such as the prevailing wages statute which predated the collective bargaining process, are an example. A proposal pending before the New York City Council would establish the following standards for impasse panels: (1) comparison of the wages, hours, fringe benefits, conditions, and characteristics of employment of the public employees involved in the impasse proceeding with the wages, hours, fringe benefits, conditions, and characteristics of employment of other employees performing similar work and other employees generally in public or private employment in New York City or comparable communities; (2) the overall compensation paid to the employees involved in the impasse proceedings, including direct wage compensation, overtime and premium pay, vacations, holidays and other excused time, insurance, pensions, medical and hospitalization benefits, food and apparel furnished, and all other benefits received; (3) changes in the average consumer prices for goods and services, commonly known as the cost of living; (4) the interest and welfare of the public; (5) such other factors as are normally and customarily considered in the determination of wages, hours, fringe benefits, and other working conditions in collective bargaining or in impasse panel proceedings.

Cost of living is a factor taken into consideration in almost all private and public sector bargaining.

The passage and implementation of the Federal Pay Comparability Act of 1970 is another significant development certain to affect the direction of all public service bargaining in the period ahead. Under the act the executive branch is authorized to make periodic adjustments in the pay of annual salaried government employees to bring their compensation into line with salaries paid to employees in comparable occupations in the private sector. Since the federal government encompasses virtually all occupations and job titles found at local, county and state levels, the annual comparability adjustments are bound to have a measurable impact on pay structures in these jurisdictions.

Role of the Neutral

The criteria for bargaining are related to the methods of impasse resolution and to the role of the neutral which have been discussed elsewhere in this book. The role of the neutral and the procedure for his selection are a vital part in the public service bargaining structure. The necessity of distinguishing between the government's role as a neutral in relation to the private sector, and the government's role as the employer in the public sector, suggest the necessity for alternative methods of choosing administrators of labor agencies as well as the mutual selection of grievance arbitrators, mediators, and fact-finders.

Summary

During the past decade there has been an extension of the private sector bargaining process to the public sector with some modifications to meet the needs of the public service. This is true even though there are many constraints upon government as the employer which stem from the separation of powers and statutes limiting the governmental employer's authority to bargain.

There has also evolved in the past decade a new quasi-governmental structure, the collective bargaining process itself, which has been used to develop and fashion the structure of collective bargaining laws, such as the Postal Corporation Act and the tripartite procedures of the Office of Collective Bargaining in New York City. A continuation and expansion of the collective bargaining process emphasizes the necessity for the development and perfection of orderly procedures for a structure of bargaining that can define and find answers to the question of who bargains for what, with whom, and why.

Henry W. Maier

4

Collective Bargaining and the Municipal Employer

Urban Pressures

The urban apocalypse has often been symbolized by billowing clouds of polluted air, miles and miles of blighted buildings, millions of the underemployed, underskilled and undereducated, marauding gangs of criminals on the streets, massive traffic jams, and an unbridgeable Grand Canyon between urban needs and urban resources. In magna-terms, it is all these things and more, and every mayor of every large city can add to the list; but a mayor can also envision the crisis of his city in the more micro-image of a dead cat, and the rising cost thereof.

During the past five years, the City of Milwaukee's cost of removing a dead cat from the street has increased 400 percent—from 9 cents to 37 cents per animal—and while all of our budgetary items have not increased correspondingly, this prosaic item relates to some of the pressures on the city's budget and the fiscal crisis which permeates every program from law enforcement to providing sewers, from economic development to social reform.

The increasing cost of dead cats tells something about the pressures of inflation, about the reason that property taxes increase at the same time that public resistance to the overburdened property tax stiffens, about the pressures from public employees to keep their wages in step with the inflationary merry-go-round. To some management employ-

HENRY W. MAIER *has been mayor of Milwaukee since 1960. He is also president of the United States Conference of Mayors and past president of the National League of Cities. Mayor Maier was formerly Democratic leader of the Wisconsin State Senate. In 1966 he published* Challenge to the Cities.

ees, the dead cat may well be a symbol of what they consider union resistance to economy measures such as contracting for a more economi-
cal dead cat removal service. Others may consider it a symbol of
management inefficiency. If the dead cat is not picked up it may be-
some symbolic of another affliction of the modern urban scene—the
job action of public employee strike.

To a mayor, often caught in the vortex of all these converging
forces, it is also a symbol of the need for increased federal and state action to help relieve the financial plight of our cities, and possibly for a
total reform of the way we pay for services in our cities by linking revenue sources directly to functions, and for relieving the overburdened
property tax.

FORCES OF DEMAND

A mayor, along with other budget makers in his government, recognizes a number of demanding forces that place pressures on the city's
budget.

There can be a prevailing public sentiment for certain programs
dealing with problems given high media visibility: crime or pollution
are current examples. Federal and state programs can be another
source of demand, as localities reach out for their share of money for
worthwhile purposes, but must pay the costs of the matching local
share and may be faced with whetted appetites for the program to continue after federal funds run out.

Another demanding force is the change in the physical, economic, or
social components of a community. A new industrial park requires immediate service needs. As the proportion of the central city's low-
income population increases, so do the costs of poverty—in my city an
estimated $31 million a year in poverty-linked services. Affluence, too,
can create demands when it leads to higher expectations of services by
consumers. State laws can require local expenditures—to install voting
machines, for example. Within city governments, departments create
pressures by demanding the latest technical refinements in their fields.
And, of course, there are the demands of various organized interest
groups for everything from sports centers, to downtown parking, to
summer jobs for youth.

When we consider that 70 percent of our operating budget consists
of payroll costs, it is apparent that service demands readily translate
into municipal manpower affecting the employer, the employee, and
the public. The advent of the municipal employee union and its effects
on municipal institutions and the public has become as much a part of
the troubled urban scene as the problems of municipal resources, inflation, rural immigration, urban obsolescence and development, and the
other problems of cities in crisis.

The actual characteristics of this developing element vary as much as the structure of government varies from city to city—from city manager cities to weak-mayor strong-council cities to strong-mayor cities where partisan politics is important. But the fact remains that the first, full weight of governmental unions and collective bargaining has been manifested in the municipal area, and it is here that collective bargaining has so closely involved officials, the public unions, and the public.

Understanding the Union

In the view of James Mortier, our city's chief labor negotiator, "In order to understand the impact of unionism on municipalities, it is necessary to have an understanding of the unions themselves—why they act as they do, their component interests, their power sources, and their expectations as they deal with municipal government and the public."

John C. Zinos, former director of District 48, American Federation of State, County and Municipal Employees, was recently appointed by the governor to Wisconsin's Commission of Industry, Labor and Human Relations. He says that basically the union is "an economic vehicle, but it has the same political aspirations of any other institution."

"Public employees want what other employees want," Mr. Zinos continues, and adds that things have not changed greatly since Samuel Gompers summed up the union objective in the word "more." Public employees no longer look upon themselves as "public servants," but look upon their employment as a job like that of any other worker, and at the local level they share the same pocketbook expectations.

In Mr. Mortier's view:

> It is important to generally understand union issues. In terms of chronology, the first area of union concern is with organization and recognition. This was paramount in the decade of the sixties. The passage of legislation in most states where organization has occurred, providing for orderly recognition by election, has tended to diminish this as an issue in the seventies.
>
> The other category of union issues could be characterized as substantive. The importance of the substantive issues in governmental negotiations has now escalated and assumes a paramount role in the bargaining of the seventies.
>
> The pressure of inflation, the drop in age of the work force, and the consequent interest of members has made the economic issues of primary importance. The strong drive for substantial improvement in wages, pensions, and health and life insurance are manifestations of this. If a situation of general chronic unemployment should persist for any time, a union drive for hours reductions to stimulate more employment will intensify.

The day-to-day relationship between the union and the employer is resuming a greater amount of union attention. From the standpoint of Mr. Zinos, it is important that there be people in the line departments who understand labor relations. It is not enough for a supervisor, for instance, to be just a good engineer.

Mr. Mortier points out:

> As the cost of labor packages goes up and governmental management seeks greater efficiency, management rights such as hiring, promoting, transferring, suspension, discharge, discipline, promulgation of work rules, standard setting, abandonment of costly past practices, the ability to contract out work and layoff employees will become increasingly more important as union issues in the future.

While unions in the private sector must exercise some political power to accomplish general legislative ends, with governmental unions on a local level, the use of politics can be a more direct tactic. However, in Mr. Zinos' view, political action is no substitute for collective bargaining and, in fact, may actually subvert the bargaining process. Appeals to the public at large, he says, are not collective bargaining, but rather "collective begging." The community has elected officers to bargain and they should be allowed to carry out the process.

In Mr. Mortier's view, "The number of governmental employees that are unionized cannot be dismissed as a political force even if their political activity were restricted solely to voting. In effect, this allows unions to sit on both sides of the bargaining table."

It should be noted that just as union officials often have detailed knowledge of the workings of the local government with which they bargain, there are also men in local government who are experienced in the workings of employee unions. A case in point is Alderman Fred Schallert, the chairman of the Labor Policy Committee and also the Finance Committee of the Milwaukee Common Council.

Alderman Schallert started working for the city in 1926 as a truck driver, and was active in the fight by the public employees union for recognition for collective bargaining purposes. As the union's business agent, he took part in the first strike by city employees for recognition, and bargained for the union with the city until he was elected to the Common Council.

As a business agent, Alderman Schallert says he saw only the union's side, but having sat on the other side of the table for the past eight years he can see valid points on both sides. Having also taken part in the budget process, Alderman Schallert says, "I have had to deal not only with setting and/or granting contract terms, but with the actual financing, within the very inflexible boundaries of the state-controlled tax rate."

He wishes that the leaders of the union side would suggest resources to help us finance the changes they feel are necessary as they formulate their demands.

Governmental Management and Decision-Making

When the mayor looks at the municipal manager-employee relationship from his desk as chief executive, he finds that his authority is oftentimes more symbolic than real.

In private management, final power and authority rest either with owners or major stockholders, frequently few in number, who have little desire to get involved in corporate management other than to insure profits. The paid managers thus have broad authority with very little restriction. This is not the case in government; particularly, municipal government.

The principle of checks on authority permeates municipal government. Power is divided in the traditional belief that power leads to despotism. Effective control of administration in many cases is vested in independent department heads, boards, bureaus, and commissions. Executive authority for administration and management is often diffuse. It is not unusual to find boards or commissions or other administrators, such as finance or legal officers, elected directly by the people or appointed under circumstances that make them virtually independent. Nor is it uncommon in certain states to find police and fire chiefs completely and utterly removed from any responsibility to the citizens and their elected representatives.

Thus, we read that Massachusetts courts have voided a section of a labor contract negotiated in behalf of the mayor and the council of the City of Dracut because the independent statutory powers of a police chief were infringed upon despite the fact that he was present at the bargaining table.

This fragmentation of authority can also affect the day-to-day relationship between the city and its employees and can be the root of problems at negotiating time. The mayor and the council can proclaim a labor policy on top, but it is the grass roots practice that affects the union members. Strong corporate management many times finds it difficult to control grass roots practices. In municipal management, the problem is compounded many times. There is the case of the city which had reached a workable accommodation with its union only to find itself put in an extremely embarrassing and difficult position by one of its independent boards having control over certain day-to-day operations which chose a different route. Without any prior warning to the union, the board announced that it was discontinuing certain operations, laying off employees, and said that henceforth the work would be contracted-out.

Since the workers affected heard of the action for the first time over television or read about it in the newspaper, it is not hard to understand the consternation that was created within the union. Nor does it require much imagination to see why the decision was difficult to implement and why the union established a high priority in subsequent negotiations for a clause to completely curb management's right to contract-out work and lay-off employees.

FISCAL CONSTRAINTS

Not only are municipal governments very much restricted and weakened in their internal management, but they are also quite limited in their scope of authority. Cities still are creatures of the state. They are not captains of their souls nor masters of their fate: "home rule" is largely a myth, and many fundamental state controls are exerted over municipal government. Controls over the sources of municipal revenues, limitations on taxing powers, various regulations concerning protection of employees that in private industry would be subject to collective bargaining are prescribed by the state.

Both state and federal neglect have contributed greatly to the fiscal plight of cities, a plight compounded by negotiating costs. It is not uncommon to read reports that the "Chicago Transit Authority must appeal to the legislature to finance money for labor packages," or, that the mayor of New York City is required to make a trip to Albany for additional revenues as a result of expenditures arising out of labor agreements. Cities such as Cleveland and Detroit have incurred deficits in their operating budgets and curtailment of vital services and layoffs of city employees are becoming increasingly common.

No labor relations agency, no matter how sophisticated or competent, can raise money when no money exists, when property tax millage limits are reached or when the rate of taxation becomes so excessively high that affluent people and industries flee the urban areas, thereby producing an even greater fiscal crisis.

The property tax is still the prime source of municipal revenue, and while there are occasional exceptions, most states have preempted for their own use other sources of revenues.

There is a close relationship between tax sources and the functional areas involved. State governments have not arrived at difficult bargaining positions because they have wide control of tax sources. The same is true of the federal government to an even greater degree. But the local government is the victim of functional disarray and is socked by all kinds of pressures, particularly inflation and the overburden on the property tax. It literally has its head at the buzz saw.

DIFFERENCES IN PRIVATE AND PUBLIC BARGAINING

If a mayor is to handle collective bargaining with great power, then he had better be prepared to be a full-time collective bargainer and forget his other functions such as planning, organizing, budgeting, and the host of programmatic tasks that are necessary for the physical, economic, social, and cultural development of the modern complex city.

The mayor is unlike the president of a private corporation in several ways. First, he has the responsibility for the total universe of a public constituency. His union constituency is of itself one of the selectors of his job. In a sense he is an employee of his own employees.

Again, public services are primarily monopolistic in character. There is no one else to supply the service and the services must be handled here and now. Many of the services are extremely vital to health and survival and even a stoppage may be catastrophic; this places great pressure on the bargainer. Too, because of the public nature of government operations, bargaining sometimes takes place in a goldfish bowl.

The diversity of services which a city provides results in a broad spectrum of occupational classes involved, often leading to a proliferation of bargaining units. (In Milwaukee we now have eighteen.)

This contrasts with the private sector where a whole industry may be recognized in a single industrial unit, or at best in but a few. Because of this multiplicity of unions, each union may try to outdo the other, creating a "whipsaw" action which can be costly.

In dealing with labor matters that have to be accepted by his legislative body, the municipal chief executive is again more restricted than the executive in private industry. This is particularly true where the legislative body has a strong check on executive power. It may look upon any substantial move by the mayor during negotiations as a policy matter which belongs within its own province. However, if the executive tries to influence the making of policy by legislators, he may be looked upon with the suspicion that he is up to some kind of political game. There are many exceptions to this statement, but it is characteristic enough to cause him great difficulty.

The municipal executive's problems are further compounded by the fact that all the while he is being kibitzed by the press. In a time of crisis the newspapers may try to pretend that he has a magic wand that can instantly solve the crisis. If he does not wave the wand he is a coward or a weakling, unlike those brave souls on newspapers who handle their own labor matters in private and perhaps fare poorly in protecting the consumer interest in their settlements. Lack of visibility in labor relations is criticized by the papers as a lack of action. Even if he works night and day behind the scenes he can find himself, as I was recently, depicted in a front-page cartoon as hiding under a desk.

SETTING UP THE MACHINERY

Practically speaking, the mayor of the large central city cannot be the full-time negotiator and carry out his other duties. However, he can try to see that the city does have a qualified professional force of skilled labor relations people and that the machinery is available within the city for the setting and carrying out of labor policy.

Some of the employees of the City of Milwaukee, as in most large cities, were organized as early as the 1920s, but wages and salaries were set as part of the legislative process by the Common Council and the relationship was an informal one without contracts.

In the mid-fifties, the unions sought a more formal relationship and pressed for the extension of state labor legislation into public employment, a move which met with success in the 1959-1960 session of the Wisconsin Legislature. Collective bargaining ushered in not only changes in procedure, but required some real rethinking of the process of government as well. The era of unquestioned sovereignty of elected representatives in labor matters had ended. Merit systems with their independent civil service commissions found that many functions, and in some instances, their very need for being, were being questioned. All of this was different and it spelled drastic change.

Realizing the implications of the changing situation, in 1964 I recommended that the Common Council set up a formal agency to deal with labor relations. This resulted in the creation of a Division of Labor Relations, headed by a labor negotiator with civil service status, and responsible directly to the Common Council. With the possible exception of Philadelphia, Milwaukee was the first to create an office of labor relations directly responsible to political authorities.

While the field of public sector collective bargaining has had great growth in the past decade, there are still areas that need development. We need more trained negotiators. We need more valid data on which to base our arguments. The simple question of how much a policeman gets paid in varying localities can get quite murky when one figure includes pension costs paid by the city and another does not. And all too often the public can be misled by the myth of simple comparison that does not take into account *all* of the variables that exist in two different jurisdictions which may affect the figures being compared. There is a need for a data bank to take account of these variables and some progress is indicated in that direction.

It is important to keep in mind, however, that no amount of expertise will relieve municipal policy makers of their responsibilities. Where these responsibilities are diffused by city structure the process is more difficult, but it is possible for the executive and the legislators to agree tacitly on goals, and then, as negotiations proceed, to modify them in the light of later developments. The task, of course, is not complete until the final document has been approved by the legislative bodies, its terms written into appropriate ordinances and resolutions, and signed by the mayor and appropriate city officials.

The Continuing Dilemma

The greatest of overriding problems for the municipal leader is the fact that in labor relations he is dealing with critical monopolies in some areas and that no weapon has been developed to firmly strengthen his legal hand in dealing with these situations on behalf of the public. It is the public itself that needs a reservoir of power to be assured of the continuity of public services. Can this overpowering fight be taken on by the public leader engaged in both developmental programs and fire-fighting on many fronts? Should this whole area be examined from the standpoint of removing it from the pressures upon elected officials and placing it in the hands of a third party public interest vehicle? To me this ought to be a fundamental part of an extended analysis.

Short of this there must be efforts to reorganize our governments— as suggested by a special committee I appointed to recommend changes in our own government—to make it possible for the public to pinpoint responsibility and hold elected officials accountable for city policies and actions. At the same time they must strengthen both the chief executive and the legislative branch so they can carry out their respective governmental roles.

It should be possible for the city to clearly spell out its policy on negotiations and to have its wage package set before it takes up its yearly budget. Too often the budget is made and the actual wages and salaries, which make up 70 percent of the operating budget, are still a big question mark. This eventually puts both the union and the employer in a difficult situation.

The state could help to clear up the situation by changing the rules which often bring about so many splintered bargaining units, frequently leading to jockeying between the units with the city caught in the middle. The role of fact-finding, I believe, should be reinforced with even better methods developed to get at the facts. State-imposed arbitration, however, I feel can be valid only if the state picks up the extra costs imposed by the settlement if they are beyond what the local government could pay. Even then, compulsory arbitration might lead to a neglect of collective bargaining by leaning on a third-party settlement.

The growth of collective bargaining has also posed new problems for the traditional municipal civil service commission. Independent civil service commissions have come under attack as being management-oriented and too inflexible in their established procedures. Many people predict that the role of the commission will either diminish drastically or will disappear altogether. Whether or not this will happen will depend greatly on how civil service adjusts to the new dynamics of municipal employment, not only in terms of collective bargaining, but also in terms of meeting modern municipal manpower needs.

Beyond all these questions of municipal employer-employee relationships, the mayor of the large city must continue to have a major concern for a reallocation of our national resources to aid our cities on the revenue side. I believe that the municipal employee has a great stake in joining this effort, for it is also his city whose future is at stake, and if the cities are not saved, all the collective bargaining in the world will not be able to produce a living wage out of their ruins.

Frederick R. Livingston

5

Collective Bargaining
and the School Board

Collective bargaining has probably grown more rapidly in public education than any other area of governmental activity. While virtually no teachers were covered by collective bargaining agreements as of the 1961-1962 school year, a survey by the National Education Association (NEA) of selected school districts during the 1966-67 school year found 1,531 separate collective bargaining agreements covering 609,034 teachers. By the 1970-1971 school year these figures had increased to 3,522 collective bargaining agreements covering 1,337,146 teachers. Approximately 60 percent of the school districts surveyed in 1970-71 had substantive collective bargaining agreements with their teachers, and 78 percent of the larger school districts (those with more than 25,000 pupils) had such agreements.[1] At the present time, 24 states have enacted statutes which require school boards to negotiate with their teachers and another 4 have enacted statutes which authorize them to do so. Furthermore, in all but a handful of the remaining states, opinions of the courts or of the Attorney General have established the legality of school boards negotiating with teachers, and such negotiations are taking place in almost every state in the Union.

FREDERICK R. LIVINGSTON *is senior partner in the New York law firm of Kaye, Scholer, Fierman, Hays and Handler. Previously special assistant to the secretary of labor, Mr. Livingston has been a frequent mediator and arbitrator in major national disputes. He is the author of numerous articles on labor relations in the private and public sectors.*

[1] Blum, *Teachers Unions and Associations* (1969), p. 106; *NEA First Annual Survey of Written Negotiation Agreements* (School Year 1966–1967); *NEA Fifth Annual Survey of Written Negotiation Agreements* (School Year 1970–1971).

School Boards Unique

This unusual expansion of collective bargaining during the course of a very few years has put great pressure on public school boards. These boards are unique among public employers in a number of ways which, quite apart from the rapid growth of collective bargaining which they have faced, make it particularly difficult for them to effectively engage in bargaining with their teachers.

SCHOOL BOARDS PERFORM BOTH EXECUTIVE AND LEGISLATIVE FUNCTIONS

Unlike most other governmental units which engage in collective bargaining, a school board is a legislative as well as an executive body. Thus in most states a school board, in addition to the executive function which it performs of administering the school system through its staff, also performs the legislative functions of raising funds through taxes, allocating these funds by adopting budgets, and setting general policies for the school district. (Some school boards, particularly in large cities, do not assess taxes themselves, but rather receive funds from the legislative body of the city or county in which they are located. The normal procedure is for the school board to prepare a budget and submit it to the city or county legislative body, after which that body raises the necessary funding by taxes and turns it over to the school board. However, even in these situations, the school board performs all other legislative functions, it being provided a lump-sum fund, which the school board then allocates.) This contrasts sharply with such governmental executives as a governor or mayor who have strictly executive functions and rely on separate legislative bodies for the funds which they spend. While it is true that in some states, village or town boards perform some executive and legislative functions, school boards are the only major spending unit of state or local government in which the legislative and executive functions are completely mixed.

To demonstrate the contrast with other executive officials, a state legislature allocates a specific amount of money for various executive functions, such as a department of health or the state police, and the governor is limited to carrying out the objectives and programs approved by the legislature within the specific budgetary allocation contained in the legislation. By contrast, a school board makes its own determinations as to how much money to raise by taxes and how the total funds available shall be allocated for various functions.

The role of a school board in the area of collective bargaining is uniquely different from the executive in other governmental areas. A governor, mayor, or other governmental executive officer negotiates di-

rectly with his public employees, as does a school board, but such negotiations are either subject to the appropriation of funds by a different
and independent legislative body or must be kept within the parameters of funding which have previously been appropriated by the legislature for employee salaries and benefits. An executive officer cannot
himself provide the funds necessary to reach an agreement. Of course,
depending on the particular relationship between an executive and his
legislative body, the executive may as a practical matter consult with
the legislative body and even try to bring its leadership into the negotiations. However, legislatures traditionally assert their independence
in determining funding levels, and hence tax rates, in this country.

The frequent role of such a legislative body is to wait until after an
agreement has been entered into between the executive and a public
employee union and then to make an independent determination
whether to fund the agreement, which determination is made through
the normal legislative process. The fact that legislative approval does
not automatically follow an agreement between the executive and a
public employee union was perhaps most vividly demonstrated by the
events which led to the strike of New York City public employees in
the spring of 1971 which ground transportation to a halt and resulted
in raw garbage floating in the city's streets. There the mayor of New
York City reached an agreement with District Council 37, American
Federation of State, County and Municipal Employees, but the state
legislature refused to provide the necessary approval for improvements
in the employees' pension plan which were a major part of the agreement. That refusal led to a strike which the mayor was helpless to prevent since he had no power to fund the terms of his agreement without legislative approval.

On the other side of the coin, state legislatures, city councils, and
other legislative bodies act similarly to school boards in levying taxes
and appropriating funds, but they do not bargain with public
employees. The problem for school boards comes because they have to
legislate like a city council but in the face of collective bargaining
responsibilities which a city council never has to deal with.

The tradition in this country is for much more public involvement
in legislative than executive decision making. Decisions which are customarily made in private by an executive official and announced only
as a *fait accompli* would arouse a storm of protest from the public and
the media if made the same way by a legislature. For the school board,
alone among legislatures, the requirement to bargain with only one
segment of its constituency—its employees—is imposed on the traditional concept of legislative availability to all constituents. This obviously gives the employees a considerably more decisive impact on
decision making, including budget and taxes, than any other segment
of the community. Furthermore, because negotiations must necessarily

be conducted in private, and since the matters subject to negotiations normally cover between 75 and 90 percent of a school district's operating budget, the decisions which most decisively affect the amount of the budget, and hence the level of taxes, are made without opportunity for parents, taxpayers, or other members of the general community to know what is happening, much less effectively participate in the decision-making process.

This obviously creates a dilemma for a school board. If it tries to keep the community informed and to obtain community views on matters at the bargaining table, the teachers' unions consider this bargaining in bad faith. On the other hand, if it does not inform the community until after it has reached an agreement with its employees, then it has failed its legislative obligation to consider the views of its constituents. It is no answer to this dilemma to say that a school board should obtain the views of its constituents before negotiations begin, for, as anyone who has engaged in serious collective bargaining knows, issues are shaped and alternatives developed during the course of bargaining. Neither is it an answer to say that the school board can bring its constituents into the decision-making process after an agreement has been reached with the employees' union and before it is finally approved and adopted by the school board. Few unions would accept a bargaining procedure under which the board's negotiator could not give assurances that agreements which he made would be adopted by the school board.

In recent years, under pressure of aggressive teachers' unions and state statutes requiring collective bargaining, school boards have generally tended to preserve the integrity of the bargaining table, thereby cutting the rest of their constituents out of the decision-making process. The negotiator for a strong teachers' union has more say in school district budgets and policies than any single person in the community, with the possible exception of the school board president and the superintendent of schools. In more than one school district, members of the board of education have first learned what the school budget would be from the teacher negotiators who had reached an agreement in secret bargaining sessions with the superintendent and president of the board. And it is not uncommon for such interested outsiders as the president of the parent-teachers association (PTA) to go to the teacher leaders to try to find out the future planning for the school system. However, the accelerating taxpayer revolt may force school boards to involve the community more meaningfully in budget decisions, which will likely result in increasing charges by unions that school boards are not bargaining in good faith.

Another difficulty for school boards which results from the fact that they are both executive and legislative concerns the application of mandatory impasse procedures contained in most state bargaining statutes. These procedures typically provide for an outside mediator to work with both parties in resolving a dispute and ultimately for an outside fact-finder to make settlement recommendations. It is hard to conceive that any of the state legislatures which have adopted these procedures would subject themselves to such outside pressure in enacting their own legislation. Yet they have had no hesitancy in doing so to school boards which exercise similar legislative functions. It obviously detracts from the ability of a school board to be responsive to the views of all its constituents when it is under pressure to accept recommendations of an outside fact-finder operating under the auspices of the state.

New York State's Taylor Law contains a particularly anomalous procedure which demonstrates the basic difference between school boards and other types of governmental units which ordinarily bargain with employees. Section 209 of the Taylor Law provides that in the event fact-finding recommendations are not accepted, the chief executive officer of the government involved shall submit them to the legislative body of the government involved together with his recommendations for settling the dispute and that the legislative body shall conduct a hearing at which the parties to the negotiations explain their positions after which the legislative body shall take such action as it deems to be in the public interest. This procedure makes sense when applied to the normal situation where the legislative body has not been a party to the negotiations and is sitting in independent judgment of the bargaining positions of the executive and the employee union. It makes no sense at all in the peculiar school situation in which the school board itself, in its executive capacity, has been bargaining with the union and then is supposed to put on a new hat and sit, in its legislative capacity, as a judge of the positions taken during bargaining.

SCHOOL DISTRICT BUDGETS MUST BE SUBMITTED
FOR TAXPAYER APPROVAL

In many states school budgets must be submitted to the voters for approval; indeed, they provide the only instance in which a protesting taxpayer can vote directly against an increase in his taxes. This is another unique problem for a school board in that even after an agreement is negotiated with employees, its budget implications must be scrutinized and approved by the voters. Consider the dilemma of a school board which has entered into a collective bargaining agreement with a teachers union, has provided the necessary funding for this agreement in its budget, and then has the budget voted down. I am aware of a very few instances in which a school board faced with such circumstances was able to go back to the teachers union and renegotiate a smaller package which then received taxpayer approval in a subsequent vote. In these instances the teachers were convinced that their long-term interests in obtaining community support, and in the indirect effect on their working environment if the budget were cut in other areas, justified the renegotiation. In most instances, however, teachers' unions in this circumstance adamantly insist that they have made a deal with the school board and the school board must live up to it. This, of course, is a most understandable position since it is very difficult to conduct negotiations if an agreement once made is not adhered to by either side to the negotiations. In such a case, the school board is faced with the choice of either trying to renege on its agreement with the teachers or trimming its budget in other areas, even though it considers those areas vital to the education process. Also, it probably would not have agreed to so large a package for the teachers had it predicted the impending budget defeat. My experience is that faced with these difficult choices, school boards grit their teeth, cut other areas of their budget, and hope for the best.

THE BROAD SCOPE OF BARGAINING IN SCHOOL DISTRICTS

The scope of what is negotiable tends to be considerably broader in school districts than in other units of government. Most state statutes which require government units to bargain with their employees define what is negotiable by adopting the language of the National Labor Relations Act (NLRA): "terms and conditions of employment." However, that language can have very different meaning depending on the situation to which it applies.

The NLRA language is often interpreted more broadly in school situations than others for two reasons. First, teachers generally desire to bargain over a much broader range of matters, including fundamental policy decisions, than most other public employees. This is because they are all professionals and hence have an interest in and expertise about many policy decisions which nonprofessional employees would not. Second, many decisions which would have no effect on the terms and conditions of employment of production of clerical workers do have a significant effect on the conditions of teachers. For example, a clerk in a typical government bureau works from 9:00 a.m. to 5:00 p.m. If there are fewer fellow clerks working with him, this simply means that work is turned out more slowly; it does not result in more burdensome working conditions for the clerk. On the other hand, fewer teachers means that each teacher has a greater load of students and this does affect the conditions of his employment. Thus it is not uncommon for teachers to negotiate such matters as limits on class size, the number of special teachers for such subjects as remedial reading, art or music, and the availability of substitutes and paraprofessional help. While the teachers' concern about these areas is understandable, and many of them probably are within the ambit of "terms and conditions of employment" in the peculiar education field, it is most unusual for these types of subjects to be the subject of negotiations outside a school district. Indeed, some teacher unions take the position in light of the severe financial difficulties which many school districts are facing that a decision as to cutting back positions or eliminating programs for economy reasons so affects conditions of employment that it is negotiable. Even the most militant unions outside of the teaching area have not thought that the decision whether to abolish positions was negotiable. For instance, in early 1971 both the governments of the State of New York and New York City eliminated large numbers of positions. The unions representing their employees did not take the position that the decision to do so, as distinguished from the impact of the decision on the employees, was negotiable. But as soon as a school district tried the same thing, it was brought before the New York State Public Employment Relations Board and charged with refusal to bargain. (The Board ultimately found that the decision to reduce positions was not negotiable in *Local 280* v. *New Rochelle School Board,* 1971.)

To take another example, the effectiveness and satisfaction of a teacher depend to a considerable degree on the ability of his fellow teachers who are sharing the teaching responsibilities for the same children with him, and the competence of his superiors. Thus many teacher unions have been demanding to negotiate over such matters as the hiring of new teachers, the granting of tenure, and even promotions to supervisory and administrative positions. Some school boards have countered that they would agree to such proposals if the teachers accepted a procedure such as merit pay to gear each teacher's salary to his effectiveness and productivity. I know of no teacher unions that have accepted such a counterproposal, although I do know of two school districts, both with excellent reputations and located in the New York City suburbs, that have given teachers a role in the decision making in these areas. Again, this is largely unheard of outside of the school field.

Other examples of subjects which teachers, unlike other public employees, commonly seek to negotiate over are curriculum, program content, funding levels of various programs, the use of money obtained from the federal government, and criteria for grading students. These obviously go well beyond the traditional wages, fringe benefits, and hours of employment. Many of them are fundamental school district policies. Yet there can be no doubt that teachers as professionals have a serious interest in these types of questions and are qualified to deal with them.

As the definition of what is negotiable in the school context expands, and decisions about basic policies for financing and operating the school district are placed on the bargaining table by state law, the dilemma of school boards pointed out above is magnified. If a school board adopts the traditional methods of bargaining as to all those negotiable items, then the community which it represents will be shut out from almost all important decisions. Yet to the extent that school boards dilute the bargaining process by involving the community in matters which importantly affect teachers' working conditions and which state law requires a board to bargain over, there will be an unsatisfactory relationship between school board and teachers union. Where school boards draw the line, or where the line is drawn for them by state agencies charged with administering collective bargaining statutes, will have a vital effect on the relative influence on decision making of teacher unions as against the influence of taxpayers, parents, and other community groups.

THE DIRECT RELATIONSHIP BETWEEN TEACHERS AND THE COMMUNITY

Another important difference between school districts and other units of government is the unusually close and direct relationship between a school board's employees (the teachers) and the consumers of its product (parents and children). While the increasing militancy of teacher unions dilutes the impact of parents on school board decisions, there continues a direct personal relationship between teachers and parents which is probably unique among government employees and the people they serve.

Ordinarily a parent personally knows his child's teacher and meets with that teacher on a number of occasions each year to discuss the child's progress. Furthermore, teacher and parent are in regular, informal contact through the child. And many parents are actively involved in school affairs through PTAs, as school lunch assistants, or in similar capacities. Because of this, the relationship between teacher and parent is usually direct and often intense—a quite different situation from the average government employee who rarely develops such a relationship with members of the public. Furthermore, parents take a much greater interest in schools and the way they operate than other members of the public do in governmental services which they receive.

Depending on the particular school district, this relationship has resulted in one of two opposite situations, either of which creates unique problems for a school board in negotiations. In most communities the relationship between teachers and parents is friendly and cooperative, and the teachers attempt, often successfully, to enlist parents on their side in negotiations with a school board. It has not been uncommon for PTAs to endorse teacher bargaining positions and even to march with teachers in demonstrations and picket lines against the school board. In one western Massachusetts community the teachers' union printed the home telephone numbers of school board members in a newspaper ad and urged parents to let them know their position on an impending strike. The board members' desire to halt the torrent of abusive telephone calls at all hours of the night probably had as much to do with bringing about a settlement as anything else. Such situations require a school board to make the difficult choice whether to "live with" parent opposition or to attempt to drive a wedge between teachers and parents and win parental backing for its side of the dispute. In such a situation the school board is faced with a Hobson's choice. Clearly a close and cooperative relationship between teachers and parents improves the quality and effectiveness of education in the schools. Yet a clever teachers' union can utilize this relationship during negotiations to put enormous pressure on a school board to accede to its demands. But successful counteraction by a board to denigrate the teachers in the eyes of parents and otherwise attempt to reduce parental support for the teachers might well, after the negotiation dispute is over, cause a long-term disruption of the teacher-parent relationship. This would reduce the effectiveness of the educational system which it is the board's primary purpose to improve. Needless to say, during the crisis of negotiations it is extremely tempting for a school board to "fight fire with fire" and many boards have deliberately turned parents and other community groups against teachers to the long-term detriment of the school system.

The other situation which sometimes develops from the strong interest and involvement of parents in schools is a community hostility to teachers. Parents then conceive of their role as fighting against the teachers for effective control of the schools. The bitter and prolonged teacher strikes in New York City in 1968 and Newark, N.J., in 1971 are dramatic examples of this situation. Here again it is extremely tempting for a school board to enflame this hostility so as to use the community as a weapon against teachers in negotiations. Yet it is hardly disputable that such hostility has a long-range negative impact on the quality of education in the school system.

On balance it would seem that a school board's primary obligation to deliver the most effective education within its resources militates against the temptation to encourage parent or community hostility toward teachers even when teachers are attempting to use parents to pressure a school board during negotiations. Certainly once the subjects being negotiated have become public, a school board should explain and justify its positions as clearly and persuasively as possible to the community. But it should avoid any attempt to denigrate the teachers or to create friction between teacher and parent. No doubt such a policy puts the teachers in a somewhat stronger bargaining position than they would be otherwise. However, in my view, the long-term benefit to the school system from such a policy outweighs any temporary disadvantage.

TEACHER STRIKES

Many of these same considerations create difficult choices for a school board in determining how to respond to a strike by teachers, which is illegal in almost all states. School boards have the same problem as other public employers in that it is virtually impossible to enforce this strike prohibition against a well-organized and determined union. Although courts invariably grant injunctions prohibiting such strikes, teacher unions seem almost as invariably to defy them. What is a unique and separate problem for school boards stems from the peculiarly direct and sensitive relationships discussed above between teachers and their pupils and parents of pupils. Thus even though it may be impossible for a public employer to stop a strike through legal action, most public employers avail themselves of all available sanctions to put the maximum pressure on a union to end a strike and settle the dispute. This can include such measures as injunctions, the violation of which can lead to fines and jail sentences for contempt of court, direct fines imposed administratively if authorized by statute, suspension, loss of tenure, and even loss of job.

However, because of the teacher-student relationship, school boards must consider that imposing such sanctions can cause long-term harm to the school system well beyond the risk that other government employers take by similar action. For example, a student's respect for a teacher, and thus the teacher's effectiveness in dealing with him, can be seriously impaired if that teacher is held in contempt of court or given even a short jail term. Particularly with younger students, any action by a school board that makes clear that his teacher is violating the law can be upsetting. This danger was vividly demonstrated by an old "Peanuts" cartoon showing Linus racing for his security blanket upon learning that "Miss Othmar," his teacher, was fired for striking. Of course, it is easy to say that teachers should not strike if it is against the law. Unfortunately, they often do, many times on at least the publicly stated ground that they are only trying to improve the system for the children. Witness the slogan of the striking Los Angeles teachers in 1970: "Teachers want what children need." A school board must think twice in such a situation before trying to explain to students, who work with the teachers every day and respect them, that they are really criminals violating the law to line their own pocketbooks.

Indeed, there is great pressure on a conscientious school board to avoid even those strikes which it could win. Uniquely in the school area the strike itself can impair the effectiveness of teachers with their students. In addition it creates personal bitterness among colleagues who take different positions as to the strike and friction between teachers and administrators who have to work with each other daily on a professional level. One of the most important factors in the effectiveness of a school is the spirit and atmosphere in the building. Obviously this is a fragile thing which can easily be destroyed during a strike, and once destroyed can be extremely difficult to recapture. This consideration has led many school boards to give in to teacher demands which they considered unjustified and which they could have resisted in a straight test of power.

OTHER FACTORS

Finally, there are a number of less fundamental but significant factors which are also unusual among government employers and which add to a school board's difficulty in handling negotiations. School boards are traditionally composed of lay persons who have no professional expertise in the field of education; thus they must rely, probably more than most governmental executives, on the advice of their professional staff. Yet a school board's chief of staff, the superintendent, is not completely the school board's man. By statute in many states he is given a legal independence from the school board, and by tradition and the ethics of his profession, he is expected to exercise that independence. In many states a school board cannot grant tenure to a teacher even if it desires to do so unless the superintendent recommends it. Under New York State's Taylor Law, in the event of an impasse in negotiations, the superintendent is required by law to make his own independent recommendations for a settlement.

Even though the superintendent is an employee of the school board and acts as its agent in the negotiations, experience has shown that some superintendents do not hesitate to make recommendations that are markedly different from the bargaining positions of their boards. Indeed, many superintendents are members of the same professional associations as teachers, and in many ways they are considered by the profession itself as more closely aligned with teachers than with school boards. And, of course, most superintendents were at one time teachers and many of them retain close ties with their former colleagues.

Furthermore, school board members are traditionally unpaid and have full-time jobs by which they earn their living. Thus unlike other governmental executive officers, they are not continuously involved in operations, and are not familiar with the day-to-day functioning of the school system. It is often difficult for them to assemble on short notice or on a continuous basis for crisis decisions during a period of intense negotiations. This sometimes results either in delegating policy making to the staff or in putting off decisions and thus exacerbating relations with teachers and making settlement more difficult to reach.

Finally, schools happen to be the area of governmental activity in which employee organization has been most rapid and effective in the past decade. There have emerged two strong national teacher organizations which compete vigorously with each other to represent teachers throughout the United States—the National Education Association and the American Federation of Teachers. Each one is influenced in its negotiating by the need to demonstrate that it can produce more for teachers than the other. This has resulted in many places in a wide disparity in the bargaining effectiveness between a school board and the union which it faces across the table. The local union is likely to be supported by a state and national organization which provides advice, staff assistance, and even substantial funding in the event of a crisis. It is probably coordinating with other teacher unions in its area, or even statewide, to present a common front and play off one school district against another.

In most places school boards are far behind. They rely exclusively on their own resources, and often devote woefully little of those resources to negotiations, which, after all, determine the bulk of their budget. While they are very effective in joint lobbying efforts before the state legislatures, they have developed only the most minimal communication, much less cooperation, in bargaining. Incredibly, many school boards still try to negotiate themselves, or through their regular staff, without retaining competent and experienced professional labor relations advisors.

Indeed, the position of the school board in the 1970s is akin to that of the private sector in the 1930s and early 1940s. During that early period very few companies, while confronted with growing militant unionism, had experienced professional negotiators representing them. Labor relations, to the extent that they were handled at all, were under the aegis of the controller or treasurer, since labor involved cost. In some companies the problem was handled by the plant manager or vice president of operations. A special director or vice president for labor relations was unheard of. In many ways, the school superintendent today is the equivalent of the plant manager or vice president of operations in the 1930s. While they may be expert at setting educational policy and operating the school system, superintendents generally have no experience, background, or knowledge which enables them to cope with the difficult problem of negotiating with teacher unions.

Proposed Changes

Many of the difficulties facing a school board negotiating with its teachers which have been canvassed in this article are inherent in the structure and functions of a school board as contrasted with other public employers. There are no easy solutions which would ease these difficulties. However, the following proposals would help the situation.

First, on a technical level, school boards must proceed in a serious and professional manner. This seems elementary, yet many school boards do not act this way. It is inconceivable that a school board would hire an amateur to run the school system, develop a reading or mathematics curriculum, or even coach the football team. But that is exactly what many school boards do in trying to represent themselves or in picking regular staff members who are amateurs at collective bargaining to negotiate for them. With from 75 to 90 percent of the average school operating budget affected by terms and conditions of employment which are set at the bargaining table, the time is long past due for school boards to be represented by professional labor relations experts, either full-time staff members employed for that purpose or outside attorneys, or, in large districts, a combination of both.

Second, at the structural level, thought must be given to devising a workable procedure which will enable parents, taxpayers, and other constituents of the board to have a meaningful voice in school policies while at the same time preserving the integrity of the bargaining table. Although the idea has not previously been tried, perhaps this could be accomplished by providing for a citizens committee representing the various viewpoints in the community which would be available to meet with the negotiators for the school board and the teacher union at the request of either side to present the community's view on issues being negotiated. This would have the advantage to the school board of providing access to community sentiment before reaching final agreement on issues important to the community. Thus it would substitute for the hearings and other procedures used by legislative bodies to ascertain community sentiment when they are not obliged to keep the issues at stake confidential. It would have the advantage to the teacher union of demonstrating to the board community support for the union's positions where such support exists. It would have the advantage to both sides of giving the community a sense of participation in decision making and thus, hopefully, engendering community support for the final agreement which is reached between the two parties and for the overall education program, while at the same time preserving the relative privacy of the bargaining table. Limiting the role of the committee to those instances where either party requested its participation would enable the negotiators to bargain without outside intrusion where that course would be fruitful.

There are obvious difficulties in establishing such a system for community participation. The community itself would have to be convinced that it was fairly represented on the committee and that the committee had a meaningful role in the decision-making process. Also, the committee members would have to be sophisticated enough to make sure that community interests were represented while at the same time being careful not to damage the progress of negotiations by intruding too much. Of course, the particulars of such a procedure would vary depending upon the needs and particular situation in each school district. But this approach seems promising enough to warrant exploration in many school districts.

The demands on the public education system in this country are certainly increasing at the same time that pressures to hold down costs grow more urgent. Many respected educators have pointed out that the schools are facing difficult and challenging times. To meet the challenge, it is imperative that effective bargaining procedures be developed that will enable school boards and their teachers to arrive at reasonable accommodation of their views while not alienating the general public from support of the school system.

Victor Gotbaum

6

Collective Bargaining
and the Union Leader

Relationship with Workers

Upon his death, Walter Reuther was greatly eulogized. He was praised for his social vision and his broad understanding of social problems. This was much deserved, but most of us knew that unless Walter Reuther had produced at the collective bargaining table his ventures into political activities and global concerns would have been frustrated by an angry membership.

This is a lesson that most labor leaders learn. It is one thing to show workers new horizons. It is more important, however, to obtain a wage that feeds and clothes their families. If you are a dove on the Indo-China war and the worker is a hawk, he will forgive you. If his wages do not keep up with the cost of living, hell will have no fury like the worker scorned.

Thus the collective bargaining table becomes all important to the labor leader. He above all knows that a poor contract can undermine his leadership authority. On the other hand, a good contract means that many of his errors of omission and commission will be forgiven by the rank and file for years to come—or at least for the length of the contract. A union leader must grasp the importance of a good pension to his older members, for example. The employer becomes immersed in cost and funding items. To the rank and filer, a good pension

VICTOR GOTBAUM *is the executive director of District Council 37 (New York City) of the American Federation of State, County and Municipal Employees, AFL-CIO, one of the largest local union organizations in the nation. He formerly held a similar position in the Chicago–Cook County area after serving unions and the federal government in the field of labor education.*

means a secure old age, an old age free from fear. This brings about a loyalty to the leadership that is terribly difficult to challenge.

The collective bargaining table is the union leader's seat of power. This is where he makes it or breaks it. This can give him the opportunity to politically wheel and deal, and to try to implement his social visions. This, in the final analysis, is where his election is ratified.

Professors and politicians deal with public service collective bargaining in the abstract. They gimmick it, insulate it, warp it, and make it synthetic. They do everything but examine it in terms of what it means to the union leader and the men he represents. Therefore they drain the union leader's authority and force him to fight a rear guard action for the life of his stewardship.

This was painfully obvious when the commission led by Professor George Taylor did its investigation to help set up a public employee relations act for New York State.

The New York act warps the relationship between the leader and the people he represents. The law discourages unified concern over the goals of collective bargaining. Instead, it places the leader's manhood on test. He is impassed to death while his virility is challenged by punitive provisions intended to do away with strikes by punishing the union (through fines and loss of dues checkoff rights), the union leader (through a jail term), and the rank and file striker (through the loss of two days pay for each day on strike). The union leader can no longer swing freely on the side of his men. With all the dire prospects facing him and his union if a strike looms, the eyes of the press, of management, and of his fellow unionists perforce must turn to the impasse proceedings. He is thus encumbered by lawyers who have to read the fine print and interpret all the provisions. He has to strive to keep from becoming a eunuch.

It is difficult, perhaps impossible, to find a middle road. Union leaders either fall by the wayside with remarkable rapidity or become heroes in the eyes of the people they represent. They either beat the law and the system, or the law and the system beat them.

The labor movement is an institution of people. The leader is supposed to represent the hopes, the aspirations, the needs of these people. In order to deal successfully with a public service union, public service management must understand the relationship between the leader and his men.

WHOM DOES THE UNION LEADER REPRESENT?

Every jurisdiction has its own peculiarities. In the public service the emphasis is on security—security on the job, security in old age. The need is basic for most civil servants. The very nature of bureaucracy makes for slow change. The people who work within that bureaucracy are very skeptical about change and precipitous change frightens them. This must be understood when you negotiate in the public service.

Public service negotiations involve other factors that do not necessarily vary from the private sector. If a union leader represents professional workers, he must bring to the table many demands that involve job content and job responsibilities. The professional, by definition, wants a say in determining the kind of job he must do and the kind of job he can do. Therefore, an Al Shanker of the United Federation of Teachers in New York City will be bringing to the table those items that management usually regards as their prerogatives. This does not mean Brother Shanker ought to expect easy concessions, but one should understand the pressures upon him to produce a professional environment for the teachers he leads.

When one represents laborers or other blue collar workers, there is going to be a greater emphasis on money and related working conditions. So it is important to understand the work needs of the group represented by the labor leader.

THE UNION LEADER'S SECURITY

Tied in with the characteristics of those he represents and the extent of his organization is of course the union leader's job security. Michael Maye, who heads up the Firefighters in the City of New York, was once a tough and unreconciled leader of the opposition. In the role of opposition, one has the luxury of making demands that can range from the frivolous to the obscene.

When you assume leadership, life imposes a much tougher responsibility upon you. You now have to produce. However, people remember the demands you made on the previous leadership when you were in the opposition. Michael Maye, despite his courage and strength, would be inhuman if he did not face his negotiations with a great deal of nervousness. Management should understand this and recognize the difficulties imposed upon a new leader coming into an insecure situation.

Of course, it is quite different for a man who has successfully negotiated many contracts, such as the leader of the Sanitationmen's Union in New York City, John DeLury. DeLury is virtually unopposed in his union and is very popular. He can survive a mistake or two because of the gains he has brought his men. Not so a Michael Maye. You just cannot treat both men the same way.

It is very important that the status each leader has within his own group be understood. There is no set formula and each individual and each negotiation must be looked at. New leaders have special problems. A Victor Gotbaum who had to fill the shoes of a very successful leader, Jerry Wurf, is one example. After suffering through six years

of struggle for survival, he became a man in his own right after successful negotiations. The pressure on Matthew Guinan, the head of
the Transit Workers Union, was intense as he replaced the articulate
and dramatic Michael Quill in a terribly difficult first negotiation.
What an act to follow!

THE UNION LEADER IS ONLY HUMAN

Newness of leadership also brings with it another difficulty. The
labor leaders whom you know is much easier to understand than the
new man at the table. One just does not bring techniques to the bargaining table, one brings personality and temperament. I would imag-
ine it would take many, many bargaining sessions to get through the
dramatics of John DeLury and find his fierce and intelligent
dedication to the men he represents. At first blush he would be impossible. The negotiations process is a very personal affair. You begin to
know your adversaries. You understand their sensitivities, their level
of dedication, and above all their level of sophistication. There is the
rub.

Public Service Negotiations

Since I am talking from the labor leader's vantage point, I will accuse both sides of the table in the public service of being pathetic amateurs. We just have not paid enough attention to the collective bargaining process, the nuances, the skills, but above all the background.
We in a sense have responded to the disdain the rest of society has for
collective bargaining in the public service. We go along with their cor-
ruption of the process, we answer in kind, and refuse to take it seriously. We become willing participants in the collective bargaining
farce society has set up for us.

If the collective bargaining process is made unimportant, the union
will give it little attention. In the private sector the process, with all
the difficulties it entails, is accepted and even stressed. In the public
sector we pay attention to everything else. We throw in a hundred and
one roadblocks to make certain that we never reach a state of maturity
in collective bargaining. Then we add insult to injury and say the collective bargaining process will not work. How can it work when everything we do militates against its success?

In general you will find two areas ignored by most conferences, seminars, and studies on collective bargaining in the public service. One is
the problems and personalities of those who do the actual negotiating.
The other is the process itself. Instead we zero in on the very things
that inhibit collective bargaining in the public service.

THE STRIKE

It is almost impossible to define the difference between a strike in the public service and a strike in the private sector. The man who withholds his labor thinks of the damage and harm he creates. When the union leader in transportation, garbage disposal, or education takes his group out, he is concerned about how long he can keep them out. What is the damage created by the strike? What is the public reaction? What is the morale of his men, etc., etc.? The problems are identical in the private sector or the public sector.

Nevertheless, in the Taylor report which provided the foundation for the New York State Public Employment Relations Act, only one paragraph mentioned the similarities between public and private strikes. The matter was then preemptorily dismissed. Much of the report confined itself to how to avoid strikes by artificial means and how to punish those who strike.

We try to avoid public service strikes by creating alternatives to collective bargaining and by legal sanctions. We make little effort to find out why these strikes occur. So, in the final analysis, we fail.

PUTTING MY BACK AGAINST THE WALL

The establishment of formal impasse procedures in order to prevent strikes has come close to killing the collective bargaining process itself. Reliance on impasse procedures alone forces the union leader to pay a terrible price. His manhood is challenged and he is forced to be a sitting duck for the dissident sharpshooters within his own union.

The laborers in our union are a tough, demonstrative group. They love the union, they know their self-interest and are loud and clear in their demands. Almost any wage rate agreed upon by the leadership is challenged by a tough opposition at the union meeting.

Right after the Public Employment Relations Act was passed we had settled a wage rate for laborers. The leadership was understandably proud of this settlement. It was a high rate and we also had obtained valuable fringe benefits for the men. Nevertheless, at the ratification the opposition, while smaller, was more boisterous than usual. The settlement was ratified by an overwhelming majority with the opposition still shouting its disgust at the leaders of the local and at me.

After the meeting was over I was surrounded by a group of the opposition who wanted to give me their final and unhappy word. It was simply this: "Gotbaum, you could have gotten us more if you weren't afraid to go to jail."

We stop concentrating on the negotiations. We do not involve ourselves in an intelligent, tough manner. Everybody has his eye on the strike and its effects upon the union leader and therefore the union. It

would be a pleasantly constructive experience if all sides could negotiate without looking at the impasse procedures, the punitive measure,
or the strike.

FORMAL IMPASSE MECHANISMS STULTIFY COLLECTIVE BARGAINING

The negotiations that brought about the New York City Office of
Collective Bargaining (OCB) were of a tripartite nature, as is the
OCB itself. The parties were in agreement any impasse procedure had
to be impartial. There was strong disagreement, however, as to other
aspects of the procedure. I was part of a small minority of union leaders who did not want a whole office set up with a complex mechanism.
We were overruled by our labor colleagues. (I am, therefore, amused
when people call the OCB, "Gotbaum's baby.")

The reason for my stand was, the more complex the impasse procedures, the more structured the impasse mechanism, the less attention
would be paid to the bargaining process itself. My fears turned out to
be correct.

The Office of Collective Bargaining has the respect of labor leaders.
We believe its present administration has been both impartial and
competent. Its very success creates a paradox. Because of our positive
feelings toward OCB, we have placed too much reliance upon its impasse procedures. I find myself conducting a continual education
campaign with the leaders of our locals to induce them to stay at the
bargaining table and "keep the hell away from those fact-finders."

It is to the credit of those who administer the New York State Public Employment Relations Board that they too are aware of excessive
reliance upon the mechanism. It is encouraging to note that Arvid Anderson, the chairman of the New York City Office of Collective Bargaining, and Robert Helsby, the chairman of the Public Employment
Relations Board, are both dedicated to the collective bargaining
process and most anxious to see it succeed. Nevertheless, the emphasis
of the law and existence of the mechanism force us away from the bargaining table itself.

It is extremely difficult for the union leader to make points during
impasse procedures, formal or informal. The fact-finder and the
arbitrator become the men who produce. It is with terrible sadness
that I must admit Theodore Kheel is probably recognized as a better
negotiator than most public employee leaders. This is sad testimony to
the status of collective bargaining in the public service. If we cannot
produce at the table, it is therefore imperative we seek other avenues
to impress our membership. This is not to say that I oppose impasse
proceedings as such; obviously, there must be a means for introducing
impartial third parties to help bring the disputants together. But I do
say that public employee collective bargaining is virtually hog-tied into
impotence by the prohibition on strikes and the intricate impasse pro-

ceedings. Together, they make collective bargaining a third cousin seated far in the back at the nuptial proceedings.

PUBLIC RELATIONS SUBSTITUTE FOR COLLECTIVE BARGAINING

In the 1970-71 negotiations between the City of New York and the uniformed forces the economic conditions surrounding the negotiations presented almost impossible obstacles to a peaceful settlement. First, because of a previous mistake the city was hit by a parity cost item in the nature of $200 million. Secondly, the city at the time faced its worst budgetary crisis.

All of this should have been brought to the bargaining table. It would have given both labor and management a chance to work out of these very difficult trouble spots. The unions needed a catharsis for their men. The city needed to face the problems and talk to the problem. Collective bargaining is an educational process. It also allows you to let off steam. But, almost nothing was done at the table; instead both sides took to television, advertising, and the loud and dramatic press releases.

Mayor John Lindsay made his first major offer not at the table but over television. It was an offer of "a cost of living increase" but nobody knew what he was talking about: past cost of living, future cost of living, Consumer Price Index, budget director's price index? All of this should have been brought to the table, fought over, and resolved. Instead he sharpened the situation, created greater animosity, and literally destroyed any possibility of decent collective bargaining. To add insult to injury, the mayor then publicly called for compulsory arbitration, which was seconded by the ever willing editors of *The New York Times*. Aside from the dreadful mistake of calling for arbitration even before an impasse had been defined, to do it publicly was a monstrosity. It guaranteed that the unions would not respond in a positive way. This is not to say that the mayor should stay out of collective bargaining that clearly affects his budget and other aspects of his administration. In fact, I have advocated the involvement of representatives of the city council in negotiations since the council does have a responsibility and involvement. What I do argue against, however, is the rush to the TV cameras with off-the-top-of-the-head remarks that never help, always hurt.

The amateurs of the media keep insisting that collective bargaining ought to be open to the public eye. They invoke the citizen's tax burden as the major reason for this. Experts such as Theodore Kheel and Arvid Anderson know the best way to insure trouble is to bring collective bargaining into the public arena. Instead of labor and management representatives talking to each other, they will talk to the public and to their principals only. Invariably, the wrong things will be said. Management will talk of the "irresponsibly high demands" of the workers, and about how services will have to be cut back or taxes raised. Understandably the media will respond in a sympathetic way. The only problem is that the media are not responsible for the operation of government.

The labor leader now has to talk tough. The strike threat becomes almost obligatory, because he is now put in an impossible squeeze. When the union leader goes public he first must talk to the people he represents, and retain their confidence. Understandably, the public responds not to the facts of the situation but to the militant rhetoric. Everybody loses in the process, a process that has little or nothing to do with collective bargaining.

THE LESS UNION SECURITY, THE MORE MILITANT LEADERSHIP

In an open shop situation, the percentage of dues-paying members give you an indication of the labor leader's militancy: the smaller the percentage of membership, the greater the militancy. In a newly organized situation or where organization hovers around the 50 percent area, the union leader knows that he must come up with something new and dramatic or at least look dramatic, in order to increase membership. Where organization approaches the 100 percent level, the union leader can afford the luxury of dealing with issues on their merits.

In one television discussion John DeLury was magnificently stylistic and involved himself in some beautiful rank and file prose. My wife, who watched the program, queried me as to whether this was going to bring the public over to his side. I submitted to her that it would be nice for him to bring the public over to his side, but it was much more important that in an open shop situation the New York City sanitationmen were 99 percent organized. Good public will is of little help to a leader whose union is poorly organized and whose opposition grows troublesome.

In an open shop situation you do not want your contract just ratified: you want it *overwhelmingly* ratified. The opposition does not need a majority, all it needs is to keep the leadership off guard. If you lose a point at the bargaining table it is not considered by the opposition to be a part of normal bargaining. "You sold out" becomes the rallying cry for the opposition. In addition you never know how many members you are going to lose because you did not satisfy their specific desires. So you become an "irresponsible union boss" or a "pirate."

The fight for an agency shop in the public sector is almost ridiculous. Management's insistence on an open shop situation is the most counterproductive imaginable. It is to management's interest that the union be stable and representative of all the people in its unit. This would give the union leader maneuverability and flexibility. It would make him less demanding, less insecure, and less verbose. The agency shop is eminently fair; yet very few governments allow it. This makes little sense and is another example of public administration immaturity. It perhaps should be regarded in the same light as the public administrator who refuses to accept the role of management.

THE PUBLIC ADMINISTRATOR'S *Noblesse Oblige*

The union leader is often confounded and confused by the public administrator in his role as a boss. Part of it is of course the union's doing. Only in the public sector, in our country, do workers effectively help to select their own boss. If you support a man for public office, it is really tough to then turn on him and accuse him of being a bad administrator, a bad negotiator, and an exploiter of the people you represent. For the public official's part, it's difficult not to become patronizing and somewhat hurt when your former ally now turns upon you in negotiations.

It is an almost impossible break the union leader must make from political support to economic adversary. But it must be done. We cheat our members, we corrupt the collective bargaining process if we do not do this.

Time and again I will receive a complaint from the membership. "Why can't we get this from the mayor? After all, we made him." You fudge the matter by insisting that the union would have been worse off if it had opposed the mayor politically. You can also say you supported him because you wanted honest collective bargaining, but this has little meaning to most members who figure the elected politician owes it to you.

In the public service, moreover, the chief executive himself does not like to be regarded as a boss. He is after all an elected official and was put there to serve all the people. Even more important, traditionally, the chief executive dreams that he can mediate between labor and management in times of trouble in the public sector. Conversely of course, the political candidate who is opposed by a union of public employees, and is elected, poses the problem of a possibly enhanced enmity born of antagonisms developed outside the "business relationship" that exists between the elected official and the union.

Governor Nelson Rockefeller of New York State was disturbed when told that he could not be accepted as impartial in selecting the members of the New York State Public Employment Relations Board. After all, was he not governor of all the citizens of the State of New York, including the public employees? In addition did he not have strong labor support during his election campaign?

It was almost as difficult to explain to the governor as to our members that the chief executive is also the boss, that the boss could not act impartially, but would have to serve his own managerial self-interest.

When you question the executive's ability to act impartially toward public employees he understandably throws out the fact that some of his best friends are labor leaders. Union leaders, both private and public, must also be reminded that the chief executive is also a boss.

If the chief executive has the right to determine bargaining units, we have examples of the way he acts in his own self-interest. Robert Wagner, when mayor of New York City, chose fragmented, small units as his criteria for representation because he thought it would save money to do it that way. Governor Rockefeller chose a single amorphous unit and then attempted to hand it over to the Civil Service Employees Association without benefit of election. Mayor Richard Daley of Chicago tied in many units to the unions that were strong political allies. None followed the precedents established in the private sector.

If the chief executive accepted the role of boss at the collective bargaining table—whether the union had backed or opposed him in the election—it would help the union leader at the table. It is much easier to deal with a tough, competent management negotiator who can define his own self-interest. This would force the labor leader to define his own self-interest. When the boss takes upon himself the role of political leader and therefore political ally, it makes it twice as tough upon the union leader. If the boss cannot determine his role it will be hard for the union leader to do it. This will mean that nobody then can engage in collective bargaining.

LIMITING BARGAINABILITY IN THE PUBLIC SECTOR

New York City passed a collective bargaining law in 1958. Upon my arrival in 1964 I was under the erroneous impression that collective bargaining was at a mature stage in the city. I was disillusioned as soon as I entered into negotiations for some of the groups in District Council 37. The city had no negotiating team. The bargaining was carried out by an able budget examiner. The area of bargainability was circumscribed to wages and other related incidentals.

It soon became apparent that enlargement of the area of bargainability in the City of New York was brought about by strikes or threats of strikes. This is not to say that many issues were not negotiated, but more often than not they were political agreements with the mayor rather than agreements worked out through normal collective bargaining.

In many areas of the United States, collective bargaining for public employees is more of a slogan than a reality. It can be a political agreement, a narrow confinement to a single issue, or anything except an overall bargaining process on those matters which are of major concern to the union membership.

Why should the teachers be denied a say in the size of classes and the kinds of curriculum that they offer to children? These are the men and women directly responsible for the education of the child. It is foolish for management to insist it has the sole responsibility for deciding what is good for education.

Everyone knows we have absolutely no social services in the welfare departments throughout the country. The heavy workload precludes any sensitive reaction by case workers to the needs of the clients. Heavy caseloads have demoralized the staff, made for intolerably high turnover, and created a welfare structure that is both costly and inefficient. Yet social service unions are told that caseloads involve managerial prerogatives. It is obviously management's way to retain its power, but it is equally obvious that it is self-defeating.

GIVE AND TAKE: BRINGING CHANGE ABOUT

If management exerts its prerogatives and keeps many issues off the table, it is also keeping a change in the status quo off the table. The best time to extract changes is when you have to concede something to the union. If you broaden the area of collective bargaining, management not only has to make concessions but can also obtain concessions.

For years the administration under Mayor Lindsay tried to keep productivity and efficiency outside of negotiations. They also complained about productivity and efficiency all the time.

The deputy mayor for administration of the City of New York complained in 1971 that the Sanitationmen's Union refused to allow more staff to be put on during the peak load time. He made this assertion loud and clear in the public press while negotiations were going on for a new contract. The deputy mayor left out one very important point. Despite the fact that his administration had bargained with the sanitationmen two times previously, this was the first time such a request had been made of the union.

It was ridiculous and self-defeating for him to go to the press when the matter was on the table. It set the union's back up, cemented a negative reaction, and made bargaining far more difficult.

As mentioned above, change comes very hard in government bureaucracy. You cannot make changes by wishing inertia away. The collective bargaining table is the best and most constructive place to bring about these changes. But when you circumscribe labor's right to ask for changes that would benefit the membership, management falls victim to its own limitations.

The history of collective bargaining in the private sector contains magnificent examples of cooperation by labor and management in the areas of classification, production levels, work rules, manning, etc. In the public sector management seems to insist on going in the opposite direction. It avoids like the plague those practices which have been successful elsewhere.

Summary and Conclusion

As soon as the labor leader in the public sector hears of the differences between the private sector and his own, his immediate reaction is that it is an attempt at exploitation! The legislative bodies cater to the alleged differences and wind up destroying collective bargaining.

A full examination of the New York Public Employment Relations Act will bear this out. The law follows the nonsense that there is no collective bargaining in the public service, and calls it "collective negotiations." Even with a dictionary anyone would have difficulty in understanding the semantic difference. The substance of the law, however, is another thing. It studiously avoids anything which already works in the private sector.

In the union leader's relations with management, we also have yet to reach a maturity that exists in the private sector. In all probability the labor leader and the public administrator will have to live together for some time to come, certainly for the life of the contract at any rate. An honest and tough adversary relationship should exist, but it also will have to continue far beyond the moment.

Management has learned in the private sector that it is costly and self-defeating when you set out to destroy a union and the leadership of that union. Each side in the private sector has a hard-headed respect for the other.

It may seem absurd, but somehow we have to remove politics from labor-management relations in the public sector. There are good bosses in the private sector but labor does not have to go to bed with them. There are bad bosses in the private sector and labor does not have to destroy them. In fact mature minds among the leadership in the private sector know full well that an evil boss of yesterday can be an excellent man to deal with today and tomorrow. Our loves and our hates in the public sector are of an exaggerated nature that keeps us from having professional attitudes toward each other.

Public service workers will become a very large part of the American labor movement. By the turn of the century, one out of four workers will be a public servant. Intelligent leadership in this area will be good not only for the labor movement, but also for public administration, and therefore for all the citizens. It is time we gave such leadership a chance to mature.

Frederick O'R. Hayes

7

Collective Bargaining and the Budget Director

Comparatively few governments in the United States have had much experience with collective bargaining. Public employee unions go back 30 or 40 years, but even a dozen years ago collective bargaining in the public sector was still in its infancy. The position of most unions was tenuous and bargaining seems rarely to have taken on the tough, no-holds-barred stance it has in some sectors of private industry.

In a little more than a decade, public sector unions have moved into a stormy adolescence. Moreover, this has occurred during a period where group pressure generally has moved to a style of high militancy and confrontation. It would be an understatement to say that the result has made the job of the budget director more difficult and more complex. More accurately, it has made the job, at least in the City of New York, almost impossible. In smaller and simpler governments, the diagnosis is not likely to be that dismal.

There is, of course, a natural conflict of interest between the municipal union and the director of the budget. The very existence of an executive budgeting function reflects a philosophy of managerial rationalism. The budget director wants a budget that is controllable. He wants to be able to prune programs that appear to involve high costs and low benefits. He wants to be able to examine carefully proposals

FREDERICK O'R. HAYES, *former director of the budget of New York City, is now holder of the Chair of Urban Management at The Urban Institute and visiting lecturer in political science at Yale University. He has also served in the federal Bureau of the Budget, Urban Renewal Administration, and Office of Economic Opportunity.*

for increased expenditures. He wants, in sum, to be able to *manage* the budget with the minimum degree of external dictation. The unions represent a powerful external force that, at best, limits and, at worst, destroys his capacity to manage the budget.

All of the expected problems from unionization and collective bargaining have, however, been grossly exaggerated by the inflation of the last five years. It has meant that union leaders after obtaining generous, even outrageous, settlements have seen them partially taxed away by price increases. The prospect of continued price inflation becomes an important factor in bargaining. Negotiation is conducted under conditions of uncertainty—neither side being able to guarantee the value of the settlement. And the classic solution—the automatic cost of living adjustment—becomes a real speculation when competitive union settlements, in private and public bargaining, are being made in absolute dollar terms. All of this is worth saying by way of introduction because inflation has not merely increased the dollar value of settlements but also has greatly complicated the process of development of bargaining relationships. Without it, the growing pains would not have been nearly so painful.

The Bargaining Process

A big government, such as that of the City of New York, will have big government collective bargaining—and its characteristics will tend to be markedly different from bargaining in smaller jurisdictions.

In a medium-size school district, for example, the bargaining will probably be done by the superintendent and members of the school board itself—the same people responsible for managing the school system and voting the taxes to finance it. The union leader will be known personally by a substantial proportion of the union members. Both parties will have much the same awareness of taxpayer and parent sentiment and of the difficulties likely to be presented in securing approval of a higher school budget and tax levy. We can, in this situation, represent the bargaining process very easily:

This is undoubtedly oversimplified but reasonably accurate.

In New York, however, sheer scale results in significant divisions within both government and union that affect the bargaining process. Collective bargaining was initially the responsibility of the Bureau of the Budget and handled by the bureau's chief examiner. To handle a growing workload and a broader concept of labor relations, the mayor in 1966 established an independent Office of Labor Relations headed by a director responsible for collective bargaining on the city's behalf. Bargaining is hence now a specialized assignment within government. The director of labor relations and his office have nothing to do with either the management or the financing of the city—and, in truth, are unlikely to be very much concerned with either. Their role is reaching settlements.

Money is the budget director's problem, and the director of labor relations contends not at all with the real problem of limited resources but with the institutional problem of his role versus the budget director's role. The director of the budget is less a part of a unified management team than a part of the problem, an adversary not unlike the union leaders themselves. The commissioner of the department most involved, the director of personnel and, to a lesser extent, the mayor himself, all similarly tend to become problems—more than resources or allies—for the director of labor relations. Underlying the situation is the belief held by most labor negotiators that they know "what it takes" to effect a settlement and that, in the large complex public body, alleged or actual limits on available resources have no effect upon the ultimate settlement. And they are, in fact, largely correct.

Specialized role playing is characteristic of all large organizations, and there is no magic that can give them the policy homogeneity and unity of smaller and simpler organizations. In retrospect, however, I believe we could have done better by including representatives of the director of the budget and the director of personnel as members of the negotiating team attending every bargaining session. Budget and Personnel would then be exposed daily to the reality confronted by the director of labor relations. And both the latter and the union representatives would acquire a better sense of resource availability, managerial perspective, and civil service system problems.

The union leader, too, is in a different situation than in smaller governments. He will usually have a sizable dissident minority within the union which does not believe he is tough enough. He may have a growing racial minority impatient with white leadership. His leadership will sometimes be genuinely precarious and in real jeopardy at the next union election. Increasingly, he will have a bimodal membership with very different demands—the long-time members concerned primarily with retirement benefits and a younger group almost wholly concerned with take-home pay.

In addition, the larger government may have, as does New York, its own impasse-resolving machinery (the Office of Collective Bargaining) or, at least, a limited number of mediators acceptable to both sides who tend to participate frequently enough to very nearly become institutional factors in their own right.

Mediators and fact-finders in New York City have tended toward recommendations more favorable to the unions than to the city. Self-interest might dictate this result. Mediators and fact-finders are, in effect, judges hired on a case-by-case basis. A fact-finder too tough on the union is unlikely to be acceptable to labor in subsequent negotiations, while the city will rarely be that critical in view of the shortage of acceptable mediators. But beyond this, the fact-finders understand the power relationships, where the advantages are largely with the unions, and the need to produce recommendations that will result in a settlement rather than a strike. Many of the settlements criticized as overly generous represent, in fact, the recommendations of panels of independent mediators.

The bargaining model becomes, as a result, vastly more complex. The following is a reasonable graphic representation:

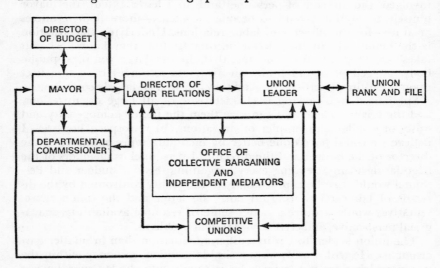

Even this ignores the city council, which in New York is ordinarily not an important factor, and the governor who can, with negotiations at an impasse, become very important.

In this complex model, the director of labor relations and the union director, both beset by other adversary relationships, are likely to represent the most compatible and comfortable of the relationships on the chart. They understand each other's problems—although the union leader's problems are apt to be the most significant in terms of settlement. Failure to satisfy them may result in a rejection of the agreement by the rank and file or a turnover in union leadership bringing in new and more difficult leaders.

But the problems of the director of labor relations are also reflected in the process and understood by the union. The most important of these is not money. It is the relationship between the salary and benefit levels agreed upon for different unions. And nothing is tougher for the city, for the key objective of a union may be the altering of the existing salary relationship with other unions. New York's 1968 sanitation strike, for example, arose partially from the belief that the line must be drawn somewhere, but perhaps mainly because the union insisted on a settlement violating the historic relationship with police and fire salaries.

The important general point is that the whole process tends to operate within a kind of internal logic and a set of standards arising from the bargaining community itself. It adapts to outside frictions if they are serious enough. A rank and file rejection of a settlement, a commissioner adamant on some work rule change, and an occasionally rigid budget director are illustrative.

State law to the contrary, the bargaining process proceeds under the implicit or explicit threat of strike, and New York is acutely vulnerable. The city could barely function during the transit workers' strike of 1966. It could survive the one-week police strike of 1971 only because superior police officers remained on the job. The 1968 sanitation strike brought the city to the verge of serious public health problems. A firemen's strike would be even worse. Even where the functioning of the city is not in jeopardy, the political viability and future of the mayor may be seriously threatened as the 1968 school strike amply demonstrated. The bias toward concessions by the city to settle are enormous. The mayor can far more easily weather the resulting money crisis than he can a major strike.

THE DIRECT COSTS

For the budget director, the first and most important effect of collective bargaining is its upward push on costs. Over the past decade, the impact upon civil service salaries in New York has been very significant as the following figures[1] indicate:

	Representative Salary		
	1961–62	*1970–71*	*Percent Change*
Patrolman	$7,331	$10,950	+49.4
Fireman	7,331	10,950	+49.4
Sanitationman	6,114	9,871	+61.4
Teacher (Board of Education)	7,623	11,210	+47.1
Correction Officer	6,694	10,950	+63.6

The cost of living increase over the same period was 29 percent. Even during the last part of the decade, the increases have significantly exceeded the rate of inflation of the Consumer's Price Index and

[1] New York City, *Budget Message of the Mayor 1970–1971*.

take-home pay of civil service workers has, in real terms, continued to increase. The Bureau of Labor Statistics reports, on the other hand, that the average take-home pay of industrial workers has since 1965 barely kept pace with the increases in the cost of living.

New York certainly has, on the average, the best paid civil servants in the country, coming a long way from the low point of the fifties. Direct intercity comparisons are perilous because of different union contract periods, the complexities of fringe benefit pricing, and variations throughout multilevel pay structures. Generally, on compensation for policemen, firemen and teachers, New York, Los Angeles, San Francisco, and Detroit tend to be close to comparable; but some other cities are, for these occupations, beginning to move into the same group. The so-called "catch-up" from substandard compensation in municipal employment is now a nationwide trend.

The editors of the *Chronicle of Higher Education* (April 19, 1971) have made an interesting comparison of average faculty compensation in American universities and colleges. Of the ten institutions with the highest average compensation, six are colleges in the New York City university system—all running ahead of Massachusetts Institute of Technology, Yale, Chicago, Cornell, Princeton, and Columbia. Two of the two-year community colleges have salary levels exceeding those of every Ivy League university save Harvard and Yale.

Whether the resulting salary levels are too high is not a question susceptible to resolution. One can urge that the job of the typical policeman, fireman, sanitation worker, and teacher is significantly more onerous and different now than in 1960 or 1965. It is clear that, even disregarding fringe benefits, New York City is paying most workers substantially more than they would earn in comparable jobs in private industry or in jobs with comparable qualifications. The private cartmen collecting trash from commercial establishments have received total compensation perhaps 25 percent less than that paid the city sanitationmen collecting residential trash. Private school teachers are often equally far below the city scale. Even if productivity in the city were as great as in comparable areas in private industry, the difference in salary level alone would lead to substantial savings by contracting out certain city services such as garbage collection.

The cost problem is, however, greatly aggravated by the enormous increase in the cost of fringe benefits over the same period. T. Norman Hurd, the New York State director of operations, reports that eleven cents of every tax dollar raised for local and state government in New York is expended for employee fringe benefits. Twenty-year retirement at half-pay, thirty-year retirement at about two-thirds pay are now standard in New York City's police, fire, and sanitation services. For the remaining civil servants, retirement is possible after 25 years' service until age 55, with a pension equal to 55 percent of pay. The 1971 state legislature refused to approve a negotiated and agreed-upon plan for 20-year retirement for these workers. The long-term trend has been to decrease the rate of employee contributions to the systems and, eventually, noncontributory retirement systems seem highly probable. The cost of pensions and fringe benefits is now approaching 30 percent of salaries.

Actuarial pension plans have typically been set up and modified only after a careful and detailed examination of costs, benefits, actuarial and investment assumptions. On the other hand, pension provisions in the collective bargaining process have sometimes been resolved within a week or even a day. It is necessary to work with rough cost figures. The meaning of various provisions is often not totally clear to all parties. It was my experience as director of the budget that most such provisions have ultimately cost New York City more than the estimates at the time of bargaining.

One wonders whether the values placed upon deferred or non-cash benefits by their recipients are as great as their costs. Some of the confusion could be eliminated by bargaining for an all-cash package per man to be distributed by the union or even by the individual workers as they saw fit. This would fix the size of the total settlement, make the price fully visible to union members, and the public, and permit the union members or the union to optimize the amenity return from the distribution of the package.

The overall effect of the substantial liberalization of pensions and fringes has been to improve vastly the lot of civil servants in the area where they have traditionally had significant advantages over their private industry counterparts—at the same time that they have surged ahead of competitive standards on cash income where they have traditionally lagged behind private industry.

Collective bargaining in New York City tends to do more for the strong than the weak. Policemen, firemen, teachers, and sanitationmen have done very well—but many, perhaps most, other civil servants have lagged behind them.

One can argue that the city need have little concern with high wages if the total costs per unit of work performed or service rendered remain within an acceptable range. The classic example is coal mining where high employee compensation justified a policy of high capital substitution which eventually made the mines vastly more efficient. This suggests that a high-wage municipal government must look for ways to reorganize and rationalize work to increase productivity. Unfortunately, the potential area of opportunity is limited. The classroom teacher, for example, at even twice current salaries is unlikely to be replaced by capital investment or reorganized into a more productive arrangement. Such opportunities as do exist have been extraordinarily hard to develop. In the absence of higher productivity, this relationship demands either higher taxes (or intergovernmental payments) or the attrition of lower priority services.

UNCERTAINTY

One result of collective bargaining in New York has been to turn budgeting into a kind of roulette game with about the same odds against winning. In some smaller communities, contracts for salaries and wages in the coming year are negotiated before the budget is prepared. In New York, the number of contracts involved allegedly makes this impossible.

The budget must consequently include reserves to cover the cost of collective bargaining agreements still to be consummated. The amounts involved are not readily identified nor are the figures for any one union easy to determine. The estimates are virtually always low— despite careful efforts—and additional funds have to be sought during the year.

Even contracts scheduled for early completion are often not negotiated on time and bargaining is extended. Some unions have deliberately kept negotiations alive until agreements with competing unions were completed.

But this is not all. Bargaining on matters of working conditions tends to pop up at almost any time—usually with the threat of job action or strike. The fire officers and correction officers have, during recent years, ultimately forced the hiring of hundreds of additional officers, not included in the budget, in the middle of the fiscal year.

And now the resolution of court cases and arbitration awards is adding to the level of uncertainty. There is a steady flow of items demanding financing not provided for in the budget. Rational fiscal planning becomes, under such circumstances, increasingly less possible.

WORK RULES AND PRODUCTIVITY

In the recently published *Agenda for a City: Issues Confronting New York,* Leavens, Bernstein, Ranschburg, and Morris comment that "in New York City, there is already in existence a system of public policy codetermination on the part of the unions." The executive order establishing the Office of Collective Bargaining reserves managerial prerogatives to the city—but it is meaningless since any resulting change in working conditions is either bargainable or subject to a labor grievance action.

In truth, few changes can be made in work organization without union approval, and it is seldom forthcoming except at a price. The powerful municipal unions are becoming the most conservative force in city government, providing the strongest pressure against change and improvement, or rational economies.

The New York City Patrolmen's Benevolent Association (PBA)

stopped, by simple ultimatum, the use of one-man patrol cars in Staten Island and the low density outlying areas of the Bronx and Queens, despite an evaluation of an experiment in Queens showing lower accident and injury rates than for two-man cars and despite the use of one-man cars in every other large city in the country. PBA also helped organize New York City boroughs to protest successfully police precinct consolidation, a demonstrable improvement in use of police time and a step already taken in most large cities.

The PBA has also successfully opposed for many years legislation permitting a fourth overlapping police shift designed to increase protection during the high crime hours. It was finally enacted in 1969. A *New York Times* article exposing the practice of police sleeping on the midnight to eight shift may have been a key factor.

The New York City Uniformed Fire Officers Association conceded only after long negotiation their acceptance of a change in the historic practice of sending three pumpers and two ladder truckers in response to every box alarm. They also agreed to the use of a limited number of part-time peak hour companies. The price was more full-time companies, unneeded in view of the peaking of fire alarms in the evening hours. The Uniformed Firefighters Associatiom bought the new approach in exchange for $1.5 million in overtime.

Sometimes, it is merely a matter of money. There is in the New York City Fire Department a sacrosanct fifteen-man unit primarily engaged in providing ambulance and oxygen service for firemen and their families at a cost of over $200,000 per year—despite city-financed health insurance for all firemen. Fifty-seven sanitation district superintendents have chauffeurs. Meals for employees of the hospitals are priced at half the 1953 raw food costs causing an annual loss to the city of $7 million.

Sewer cleaning gangs were provided for a nonworking motor vehicle operator until agreement was finally reached to substitute a working laborer as driver. All three uniformed forces are loaded with light duty and limited duty men and officers who are protected by the unions from medical retirement. The administrative separation of the provision of social services to welfare clients from the payment of benefits to the same clients in the Department of Social Services was possible only with the payment of expensive adjustment allowances to those affected.

Increasingly, workload limits and requirements are inserted into collective bargaining contracts. The contract between the United Federation of Teachers (UFT) and the New York City Board of Education establishes limits on maximum class size, provides for a minimum number of free periods for administrative and preparation work by teachers, provides for the continuation of a remedial program (More Effective Schools) designed by the UFT and since demonstrated, by evaluations conducted by the Center for Urban Education, as of questionable effectiveness in improving reading scores, and provides for $10 million for a new compensatory program of education to be designed in collaboration with the UFT.

The particulars are only illustrative. The basic point is that collective bargaining has sanctified and blessed the status quo and sometimes established new requirements on working conditions. The effect is to increase vastly the difficulty of making changes. The internal structure of government is becoming increasingly rigidified with consequent effects upon its capacity to generate change and innovation.

The problem is more subtle in some of its aspects. For example, some executives do not propose changes because they anticipate the unions will reject them. A second aspect is the unusual role of rank and file sentiment and the enormous problems faced by union leaders in dealing with their own membership.

UNDESIRABLE PRACTICES

Some elements of the collective bargaining process are particularly objectionable and can be regarded as pathological forms.

One is the increasing tendency for agreements negotiated and supported by union leadership to be rejected by the rank and file. The general attitude is apparently "what can we lose?" And, in truth, they lose nothing and will frequently gain. But it will, inevitably, make a farce of negotiation and lead untimately to initial settlements that are intended, both by union and city leadership, to be rejected and subsequently modified.

A second is the "Salome syndrome," a demand in union negotiations that the city supply the head of a third party as a part of the deal. This was most directly evident in the UFT negotiations in the Ocean Hill-Brownsville dispute where some of the district-appointed principals had to be sacrificed to achieve a settlement. But much the same principle was involved in the PBA demand that the 75-year parity with fire salaries in New York City be violated to give patrolmen higher salaries than firemen and correction officers. Relative status is becoming more important than absolute status and this means a press for settlements that are damaging, at least relatively, to a third party. This may be, generically, part of a broader and more important tendency toward the insistence on concessions that really hurt.

A third problem is less common but serious. The complex bargaining process produces strange allies, sometimes the department involved and the union. This can be most evident when the bargaining agent is the department itself as is the case with the New York City Board of Education and the New York City Board of Higher Education.

The Board of Higher Education had by resolution urged parity between senior and community college salaries when both were determined unilaterally by the city (the Bureau of the Budget and Department of Personnel). It is therefore scarcely surprising that the first collective bargaining contract negotiated by the Board of Higher Education so provides. The provision for 50 distinguished professorships was actually suggested by the board, not the union. Did the Board of Education really fight the union proposal to reduce class size or the initial proposal for a More Effective Schools Program? Legitimate doubt can be expressed. In other negotiations, ideas appear that past history indicates are close to departmental thinking. The effect is to force additional expenditures under the sanctity of union contract upon the mayor, the city council, and the director of the budget.

A fourth problem has been the tendency of some unions to seek through action by the state legislature benefits they have been unable to negotiate through collective bargaining. This has been especially true of pensions but there are cases of legislation affecting work rules and manning.

Last Words

It was a far easier world for public managers when decisions on employee compensation and benefits could be made unilaterally subject only to the approval of the legislative body. And, perhaps more important, the capacity to realize managerial objectives was far greater when management still had managerial prerogatives, when workload, work organization, and working conditions were determined, not negotiated.

There are fairer ways to determine employee compensation than either collective bargaining or managerial dictate. The use of an autonomous, quasi-judicial body operating under statutory criteria would have obvious advantages. And the effect of changes in work rules and conditions could, theoretically, be reflected in compensation determinations or resolved by grievance action before the same or some other judicial body. Such an arrangement would not, however, be a realistic rapprochement with the milieu and the human beings with which it must deal.

There are persuasive indications that the character of municipal labor relations is only one manifestation of the powerful social forces that have swept the nation during the last decade. The demands for participation and the erosion of institutional authority and of authority figures go far beyond the labor movement. Community participation and militant unionism in the public sector are clearly bed-fellows. Both, in New York, are destructive of efforts toward pure managerial rationality. Both involve a complex of implicit as well as explicit objectives—political as well as economic and, perhaps above all, the psychic satisfaction of assertion, rebellion, and extortion directed against "the system" and its leaders, whoever they may be.

But if New York City did not have collective bargaining, we might well have to invent it. Employee psychology—particularly among younger workers—strongly suggests that militancy would have its expression, probably in numerous wildcat strikes and in the deliberate erosion of work discipline. The "unauthorized" police strike or job action in January 1971 is illustrative. The collectivity and the union leader constitute a higher degree of responsibility, accountability, and commitment to negotiation than many of the employees they represent.

All of this is one manifestation of participatory democracy, one competitive with community participation. It suggests evolution toward a state of worker involvement reminiscent both of Pope Leo's *Rerum Novarum* and of Leningrad in 1917 with its slogan: "All power to the Soviets of the workers and the soldiers."

One does not have to be a budget director to see that the new militant participation has a price. And the largest price is the increased rigidity of public systems and it is reflected adversely both in productivity and responsiveness. The operative rules in an increasing proportion of the public sector in New York City seem to be approaching the *liberum veto* which immobilized the eighteenth century parliaments of Poland by permitting the negative vote of a single participant to kill any legislation.

Given our social and democratic structure, I see no alternatives to collective bargaining despite all its problems and shortcomings. We may as well recognize that the problems cannot be resolved by decree. They will have to be worked out by unions and governments. Collective bargaining has become an incremental process of social engineering which must be handled with more ingenuity, more skill, more sense of long-term direction, and a greater degree of social responsibility by both unions and governments.

Arnold M. Zack

8

Impasses, Strikes, and Resolutions

Emergence of Public Sector Conflict

The Boston police strike and the New York City transit strike occurred nearly half a century apart, yet both seem like ancient history in light of the rapid pace of events since the latter.

The intervening period was one of relative peace and quiet in the public sector. Employees were content with the merit system and job security assured by state and civil service commissions and departments of education. These protections and the higher prestige accompanying public sector employment discouraged comparison with what was going on in the private sector. Even after the 1935 passage of the National Labor Relations Act extended the rights of organization, recognition, and collective bargaining to industrial workers, there was a continuation of tranquility in the public sector.

Only in the 1960s did there begin to be felt a massive stirring of public employees as they began to object to decades of often paternalistic treatment. There were several reasons for the change. *First,* expanding demand for public service brought about a dramatic increase in public employment without a comparable rise in public income, causing a lag in public sector wages in comparison to industrial wages. *Second,* public employees began to question their exclusion from the protections afforded private employees by the National Labor Relations Act. *Third,* a younger, more militant, and more largely male influx of personnel sought to mobilize the public sector and seek

ARNOLD M. ZACK *is an experienced Boston mediator, fact-finder, and arbitrator in both public and private sectors. He is currently "umpire" for the Board of Education and the Teachers Association of Baltimore County, as well as for several other private companies and unions. Mr. Zack is also labor arbitrator and referee with the National Mediation Board.*

benefits achieved by public sector employees in other countries and by private sector employees in this country. *Fourth,* the traditional grants of prevailing wages extended to government-employed construction workers and others under the federal and state Davis-Bacon-type laws stirred the desire of noncovered public employees to achieve wages and working conditions matching those in the private sector. *Fifth,* private sector trade unions, with stagnant or dwindling rosters, began to organize state and local employees to spread their gospel and increase their numerical and financial strength. In so doing they stimulated the previously passive National Education Association and its affiliates as well as the various civil service employee groups to new militance of their own. *Sixth,* President Kennedy's Executive Order 10988 of 1962, granting limited collective bargaining rights to federal employees, was interpreted by state and local government employees as a mandate for protesting the historical denial of such rights on the state and local level. *Seventh,* a rising civil disobedience in the nation, as demonstrated in the civil rights movements, draft resistors' movements, antipoverty activities and war protests, convinced militant public employees that protest against "the establishment" and its laws was fruitful and could be a valued vehicle for bringing about desired change.

Finally, and most importantly, the demonstrated success of initial illegal strikes such as the New York transit strike and some early teachers' strikes became powerful proof that the *power* to strike was of far greater relevance than the *right* to strike. As long as some employees obtained improvements from the strike, others recognized it as a useful vehicle for their protest as well. Now even police and firemen have begun to strike with increasing frequency. These factors culminating in the increasing militancy of public sector employees have been a powerful catalyst for change. They are forcing the legislatures into varying responses as they have struggled to deal with this new outburst of public employee protest. This rapid evolution deserves attention, not only for its historical interest, but also because it provides the background for understanding the varied legislation currently on the books, and proposals for the future, all oriented toward forestalling the need for resort to the strike in order to resolve the impasses arising in public sector employee relations.

EARLY LEGISLATIVE REACTION TO THE STRIKE

The traditionally accepted concept of the illegality of the strike has provided little cause for concern to legislatures over the years. State court decisions and attorneys general opinions made it clear, if legislation did not, that the strike was illegal. Until the mid-1960s there was no need even for a program of penalties, for public employee strikes were few and far between. Even then when discharge penalties were spelled out as in New York's Condon-Wadlin Act, it quickly became evident that enforcement of the act by discharging employees would preclude operation of New York City's transit system. Necessarily this frustration led to a legislative amnesty for those involved.

The Condon-Wadlin story indicated that penalties levied against the strikers themselves were futile, and that strikers could indeed benefit from breaking the law.

The result was a recognition by New York and other states that there was a need for machinery into which employee unrest and dissatisfaction could be channelled, hopefully to do away with the need for resort to the strike. Such machinery was in fact established for public employees in a number of states, such as Connecticut, Massachusetts, Michigan, New York and Wisconsin by 1966, while several others enacted specific machinery for certain categories of public servants such as teachers, police, and firemen.

But either a lack of conviction about the effectiveness of the new machinery or, more likely, the political realities of bill-passing generally resulted in tying a prohibition of the strike to the availability of the new machinery. In New York State, still smarting from the impact of the Condon-Wadlin setback, the legislature redirected its thrust on penalties, providing penalties against the union and the union leadership, rather than the strikers themselves. We are all aware of the consequences of that tack: Mayor John V. Lindsay negotiating with convicted and imprisoned union leaders, while $10,000 per day penalties against the United Teachers Federation mounted up at a cost averaging 40 cents per teacher per day. The sanitation workers in a smaller unit bore the heavier penalty of approximately $1.00 per man per day in fines.

In the period since 1966 the public sector strike, although illegal, has come to be an increasing reality in the life of the citizen and the life of the community. The public has overcome its initial blind fear of the public employee strike, and has learned to adapt its daily living to the illegal action. In another sense this also reflects our tolerance of the growing civil disobedience of multitudinous groups in our society and our ability to adapt to various forms of disruption.

Initial strikes of public employees in the late 1960s also elicited a substantial measure of public empathy as striking teachers and others made out a case for their equitable claim to reasonable wages. But by 1972 this public empathy had begun to wane. Once substantially underpaid, teachers, police, and firemen in larger cities with collective bargaining laws have in many cases eradicated the inequities they formerly bore in comparison to the private sector; and more recently their wage rises have tended to surpass those in the private sector. The public has come to realize that the funding for these increases has come in the form of higher taxes.

MONEY ISSUES IN COLLECTIVE BARGAINING

To an ever greater degree, the public employer is feeling the pulls and strains of inflation as the public demands more services. Property taxes are frequently at their legal maximum, and cuts in state and federal financial aid further exacerbate the problem. Costs rise while income remains constant. Taxpayers too feel the burden, suffering individually from inflation, and tend to become increasingly hostile to even greater employee demands in an era of high unemployment.

The public employer has come to recognize that holding the line against growing costs of operating government is a prerequisite to his own political survival. He even learns that a strike might be a good way to cut down on salary expenses while revenues continue to flow in.

The impact of this "crunch" on collective bargaining is obvious. Employee organizations used to substantial increases based on the comparability criteria prevalent in localized bargaining except to perpetuate their past rises. The employer's response reflects the impact of the financial pressures on local and state governments. Whereas he once pleaded "inability to pay" as a guise for the more accurate stance, "unwillingness to pay," the inability-to-pay argument now takes on a truer ring. Funds may indeed not be available, nor perhaps even the ability to raise funds. Referenda for larger school and government budgets are repeatedly rejected by the tax-payers, and employers are forced to resort to reducing other programs to make money available for negotiations.

The ever tighter economic situation in communities and states magnifies the prospect of impasse in the parties' negotiations and makes the availability of dispute settlement machinery all the more important. This is true regardless of whether a wage freeze is in effect. Indeed a freeze on wages raises the prospects of noneconomic items becoming "strikable issues."

Evolution of Collective Bargaining Machinery

As a growing number of states provide leadership for the establishment of machinery to permit workers to organize and to enter collective bargaining, we find the greatest emphasis being placed upon developing a dispute settlement procedure which will effectively resolve conflicts without the need to resort to the strike weapon. The approaches and statutes have varied, but it is nonetheless possible to generalize as to the various steps set forth in most statutes. The prime objective has been to expedite collective bargaining, and stimulate settlement through direct negotiation. Let us examine the procedures in somewhat greater detail.

The laws have provided for two types of "negotiation" between the parties. The earlier and more limited legislation was of the "meet and confer" type such as that adopted in California and other states where the employer was obligated to provide opportunity for employee organization representatives to set forth employee requests and positions on various items. Although this did provide a breakthrough in the sense of imposing upon the employer a requirement of confrontation with the employee's representative, it fell short of institutionalizing the give-and-take between parties which is necessary for true negotiations. Certainly the employer was free to partake in such "horse trading" if he wished, but when the crunch was on and he had unsuccessfully met and conferred with the employees' representatives, he was free to introduce unilaterally the wages, hours, and working conditions he believed appropriate.

A more liberal approach was that taken by states which called for negotiations as nearly comparable as possible to the collective bargaining which had become the backbone of employer-employee relations in the private sector. Public employers were thus authorized and required to enter into good faith collective bargaining with the objective of achieving accord on wages, hours, and working conditions. The analogy to the private sector provided a valuable stimulus to the parties to engage in the form of bargaining most conducive to achieving mutuality.

Obstacles—But at the same time there have been obstacles to complete comparability to collective bargaining in the private sector. The first is the general absence of an effective system of penalties for employers and unions who fail to make the necessary good faith effort to achive agreement. In the private sector the National Labor Relations Board (NLRB) exercises a watchdog role imposing penalties upon the employers and unions who fail to bargain in good faith. Although such sanctions might be equally appropriate for imposition on recalcitrant parties in the public sector, legislatures have generally shied away from authorizing them, and indeed, in most state jurisdictions the legislation does not even provide for a supervisory agency such as the NLRB.

The second, and more obvious, weakness of the public sector analogy to private sector collective bargaining is the general prohibition of the right to strike in the public sector. The absence of the right to strike in the great majority of jurisdictions has permitted the employer to bargain with the assurance that if his offer is not acceptable, the employees are legally prohibited from asserting the same economic pressure as might their private sector counterparts. This assurance has been further strengthened by the fact that the strike bar often has severe penalties tied to it. Despite this burden, the growing militancy of public employee organizations is forcing collective bargaining into a format more and more akin to the private sector as increasing numbers of public employee organizations risk violation of the law by illegal strikes to attain favorable wages, hours, and working conditions.

Despite these possible weaknesses of public sector bargaining, the fact remains that it has been largely successful as a device for assuring the employees a strong voice in determining their working conditions, and for insuring the employer and the public that its employees are working under conditions which are acceptable and mutually agreeable.

The means of achieving such agreement vary widely, running from direct agreement between the parties themselves, without any outside participation, to agreements arrived at after a whole sequence of appeal steps, including, perhaps, mediation, fact-finding, superconciliation, and even binding arbitration.

DIRECT NEGOTIATION

Direct negotiation, is, without doubt, the most desirable format for dispute settlement; for if there is to be a workable agreement, it must come directly from the partners to the relationship. Even if there is outside neutral intervention through recommendations, or an arbitration award, such reports are not self-initiating or self-enforcing and, in the last analysis, must be acceptable to the parties themselves before implementation. Thus, since the parties must finally accommodate to language with which they must live for the period of the agreement, direct negotiation remains the keystone of collective bargaining.

Nonetheless, it must be recognized that hostility between the parties, or inexperience, will sometimes preclude effective direct negotiations. One or both of the parties may become so emotionally embroiled in the dispute that it is incapable of altering its position to meet the legitimate needs of the other side. Similarly, there may develop a personal antagonism by one or both of the parties' spokesmen, in which personal venom replaces responsibility to the union membership, the government agency, or the taxpayers, and thus stagnates communication as well as movement between the parties. Inexperience or naïvéte is also a reason for direct negotiation failure. Either party may inadvertently escalate the dispute by failure to respond to the right clue from the other side, or to judge properly the consequences of escalating the dispute beyond the direct negotiations stage. This possibility of failure is universal in negotiations. It occurs in the private as well as the public sector. In the private sector the pressures for direct settlement are perhaps greater with the legal strike lurking in the background. In the public sector the pressures are not so great, not only because of the somewhat reduced likelihood of the strike, but also because of the ready availability of an increasingly long ladder of appeal devices.

In other words, the absence of appeal machinery may itself be an incentive to facilitate settlement. If there is no prospect of a place for appeal, and uncertainty as to action or attitude if settlement is not achieved, this may of itself encourage settlement. On the other hand, the availability of appeal machinery may indeed stimulate appeals in the expectation that third party intervention might get either side "off the hook," or perhaps, exact a "little bit more" than could be achieved through voluntary settlement. This prospect of appeal also tends to freeze the parties in their initial positions for fear that any concessions toward settlement might be viewed by subsequent intervenors as admissions of weakness on the subjects in dispute. This tendency to adhere to initial positions and to hold back on offers of compromise is the antithesis of voluntary dispute settlement. Indeed, the amount held back for the appeal might be adequate to achieve a settlement without appeal if offered in direct negotiations.

If a jurisdiction does not provide for a formal impasse procedure, the parties are free to negotiate one between themselves, provided that collective bargaining is authorized for the state. Such self-developed procedures benefit from a positive orientation of the parties toward settlement, and are likely to be more effective than if one of the parties is dragged screaming into an appeal procedure that it considers imposed from on high.

TYPES OF APPEAL MACHINERY

The success of any machinery is related to the extent to which the parties voluntarily accept it. Thus as direct negotiation is more desirable than third party intervention, mediation or conciliation with its emphasis on voluntarism must be deemed to be more desirable than fact-finding. And fact-finding, since it is advisory and requires consent of the parties for implementation of any recommendations, is considered more acceptable than binding arbitration. The distinction between these various appeal steps must be clearly recognized:

In mediation or conciliation, the neutral functions as an extension of the direct negotiation process. By separate and joint meetings with the parties, presumably maintaining the confidence of each side, he seeks to expand the area of agreement until all disputed items are resolved.

In fact-finding, as that term is used in the public sector, the neutral functions in a more judicial role, receiving in joint session evidence from the parties in support of their respective positions, permitting examination and cross-examination of witnesses, until he has collected sufficient evidence to prepare a report of his findings and his recommendations for settlement.

In arbitration, the judicial-type procedure also prevails, but the arbitrators' findings are final and binding on the parties rather than advisory, as in fact-finding.

In both fact-finding and arbitration there may be a tendency for the neutral to attempt some mediating, presumably with authorization of both parties. This may result in an agreement, but, at the very least it permits him to ascertain if his advisory or binding findings lie within the range of acceptability of the parties. For it must be remembered that unlike private sector use of interest arbitration or even fact-finding, its use in the public sector is imposed rather than voluntary, and compliance with the findings much more tenuous.

Let us look at each of these intervenor procedures in turn to assess their strengths, weaknesses, and relative effectiveness.

MEDIATION

Mediation by federal and state government agents has become accepted as an effective means of resolving disputes between labor and management in the private sector. It has been introduced into the public sector in the expectation that similar success in achieving settlement will occur. When public sector mediation was first proposed, there was fear that utilization of government employees as mediators would contradict the concept of impartiality since the mediator would be an employee of—and thus presumably beholden to the employer— the government, even though employed by a different level of government. There was also hostility over the location of the mediation service, the employers distrusting a mediation service housed in a department of labor while employees, such as teachers, resented its location in a state department of education. The parties did learn to live with these difficulties in several states. Unfortunately, however, in states where the public sector mediation function was given to a staff already engaged in private sector mediation, the responsibility often fell on an already overworked group, with little or no prior experience in public sector bargaining. The problem was intensified by the seasonal congestion of public sector disputes as all communities sought to complete contracts prior to statutory deadlines.

Public sector mediation tends to be quite different from private sector mediation. This is true for several reasons: First, the private sector mediator works in the context of a free labor market, business competition, profit levels, and the like. These factors are not controlling in the public sector where tax structure, legislative controls on budgets, state aid formulae, and civil service rules tend to be more pertinent standards. The mediator must learn to work within a context that forbids the employer from going out of business or immediately passing on the increased cost of settlement to the consumer. Second, the issues in dispute tend to be quite different from the traditional private sector problems of wages, hours, seniority, and the like. The public sector mediator must learn not only a wholly new vocabulary, he must also learn to deal with questions of classroom size, tenure, curriculum development, police-fire parity, and the like. Also, the mediator must learn to work within the context of the illegal, although perhaps equally realistic, strike threat. Even with the reality of the public sector strike, the public sector mediator must still operate within the context of possible fact-finding and perhaps even binding arbitration over new contract terms, which tends to dilute his effectiveness.

Those states which have established new agencies are confronted with the seasonality of public sector disputes and resultant difficulties in scheduling. Throughout the year staff mediators are able to handle a steady inflow of disputes, but when many come in at once the result has sometimes been shoddy efforts. The process is narrowed to single visit efforts, or must be carried out within an agency limit of four or five meetings, after which the mediator is pushed to declare the impasse unmediable and ready for the next impasse procedure step. This is not only penny-wise and pound-foolish in terms of the added and perhaps unnecessary costs of fact-finding, but it is also contrary to the more preferable goal of having the parties learn that they can best work out their conflict alone or even with a mediator.

The seasonality problem is overcome in some states by utilizing the services of outsiders whom the state agency believes have the competence and acceptability to function effectively as mediators. The tendency has been to try to utilize the services of private sector labor-management arbitrators, but these individuals are generally extensively booked in advance with better-paying private sector work to do; are often unwilling to work the long hours and night sessions associated with mediation; and reluctant to travel to the out-of-the-way communities where the mediation often takes place. Although many arbitrators have had prior service as mediators, the skills are in fact quite different, and there are some highly acceptable arbitrators who have difficulty attaining acceptability as mediators.

As noted by William Simkin, former director of the Federal Mediation and Conciliation Service, in a speech to the 1970 meeting of the National Academy of Arbitrators:

> A successful arbitrator makes his living by making decisions. Because this is so, the arbitrator-mediator instinctively develops quite quickly his own concepts of good solutions. But decision making on the issues is not a basic mediation function. It is the parties who make the decisions. Any too-ready propensity by a neutral to make tentative decisions in his own mind or recommendations on the issues to the parties can be fatal . . . The hard fact remains that the adaptation of an arbitrator to the mediation function is not an easy transition.

Some state agencies have sought to fill the gap by calling into service individuals who have had prior experience in the affected government service. Unfortunately, the prior experience of those used was usually on one side or the other. This compounds the individual's handicap of inexperience as a mediator with problems of acceptability.

Although state statutes do frequently provide for mediation, and do make mediators available without charge to the parties to help resolve the impasse, there are many communities, including those in jurisdictions with state-provided mediation services, which have opted to establish their own mediation step. In this way they are assured of selecting an individual who is mutually acceptable as mediator. The process usually utilized to establish such private machinery is for the parties mutually to select an individual, or failing such agreement, to request the American Arbitration Association to submit a panel of candidates to each party from which they in turn can designate their highest mutual choice. This private selection system has the additional "advantage" of the parties jointly paying for the services of the mediator as an additional inducement to direct settlement.

EXPANDING USE OF MEDIATION

The evidence indicates that public mediation is on the increase. Not only are direct settlements becoming more difficult to attain, but more and more employee organizations hitherto inclined to accept employer offers (as they did prior to collective bargaining legislation) are learning they can get "a little bit more" through the appeal procedure. At the same time the economic pressures of the inflation, reaching of taxable limits, and the incipient taxpayer revolt are strengthening the resistance of employers to give in to employee demands they might earlier have acceded to. The move to more mediation is also made quite likely by the fact that more and more states are undertaking to establish mediation procedures as part of their dispute settlement machinery.

POTENTIAL SHORTAGE OF MEDIATORS

Mediation will probably be required in areas where there are few, if any, individuals with either management-labor backgrounds or mediation experience. Reliance on the relatively small cadre of experienced labor-management experts and/or mediators currently located in the industrial belts of America, unwilling to travel too far, unwilling to work the hours requested by public employers and employees, and in average, too aged and too successful in their private sector practice to be even interested in public sector mediation, clearly will not produce an adequate supply of neutrals to meet the needs of the situation, particularly as more rural states enact mediation steps for their public sector disputes.

The easiest way to solve the mediator shortage is, of course, for the parties to settle directly, obviating the need to resort to mediation. Another deterrent to the use of mediation might be to charge the parties for its use, rather than to provide it as a free service as at present. But if mediation is to be used, two aids to conservation of mediators suggest themselves: One is to reduce the number of bargaining units of amalgamation of districts or, hopefully, negotiation at the county, regional, or statewide level for local services. Although local variations in conditions might still require local adjustment, statewide determination of economic issues would take much of the hostility away from the local negotiations, thus strengthening the likelihood of direct settlement of those remaining noneconomic issues.

A second conservation technique would be to better stagger the need for mediators by moving away from the seasonal negotiating crisis. This could be done by legislation establishing different budget deadlines among various communities, or by creating staggered legal deadlines for contract settlement in a number of communities, with penalties such as reduced state aid being imposed upon those communities who are unable to resolve their impasse prior thereto. The prospect of a smaller pie to divide may be enough to trigger more sincere bargaining. Additionally, efficient utilization of the skills of state agency staff mediators could be achieved by removing them from routine administrative tasks such as conducting elections and by contracting out various quasi-judicial functions which they must often exercise at present, such as ruling on unit determinations, conducting certification elections, ruling on disputed elections, and the like.

Even by employing the foregoing suggestions, it is clear that an inadequate number of mediators will be available to meet the expanding demands of mediation as it permeates those areas of the country now without public sector dispute settlement legislation. It would appear unwise for a state legislature to enact a requirement of mediation without assurance of available, competent mediators to carry out the task. This would suggest some form of training effort be undertaken to equip potential neutrals with some of the techniques used in effective mediation. The Federal Mediation and Conciliation Service and some state boards have established training programs for their own personnel, and expansion of such activities to cover other jurisdictions would be fruitful.

Fact-finding

As indicated above, mediation—as a continuation of the parties' direct negotiation process—has the greatest potential for stimulating voluntary settlement between the parties. This has been the effect in the private sector where the almost exclusive alternative to settlement is the economic pressure of the strike. If the strike or lockout were legalized in the public sector as the alternative to settlement at mediation, this would most certainly tend to increase the number of settlements in mediation. But the trend of state legislation has generally discounted mediation as the finality, and instead incorporated an appeal step of fact-finding. This was intellectually appealing to draftsmen as the *quid pro quo* for denial of the strike right. As originally hoped for, the parties would be forced to accede to the fact-finder's proposals since the strike and lockout were forbidden and therefore presumably would not occur. Fact-finding has, in fact, come to be accepted as yet another appeal beyond mediation. It is evident that the parties increasingly seek to utilize all the available steps of the procedure, to get their "little bit more." The very availability of fact-finding tends to assure its invocation, and consequently diminishes to some degree the likelihood of settlement in mediation. Mediation, with fact-finding waiting in the wings, sometimes takes on the appearance of a rite which must be gone through before the parties get to real crisis bargaining. The problem is made somewhat worse by the fact-finder's tendency to delve enthusiastically into what transpired at mediation so he can gauge the area of acceptability of his own report. If this happens in one year's impasse, it assuredly will lead the parties the next year to hold offers of compromise close to their chest during mediation, recognizing that they will have to yield even more when they get to fact-finding, or beyond.

LIMITING APPEALS TO FACT-FINDING

Unquestionably the effectiveness of mediation would be improved if fact-finding were not so readily available, or if appeal to it involved some risk that the parties would not do as well as they might have done in mediation. Several ideas to accomplish this suggest themselves. First, prohibiting the fact-finder from taking evidence of what transpired in mediation sessions might accomplish this goal. By preserving the sanctity and privacy of the mediation effort, it might increase the likelihood of its sincere use and success, and provide the prospect of greater risk in invoking fact-finding than before.

Second, making the parties bear the cost of the fact-finding effort, as in New Jersey, would also tend to stimulate settlement in mediation. Where fact-finding is free, there is no need to calculate whether the "little bit more" that is sought will indeed offset the cost of invoking the procedure itself. In this regard another encouragement to more effective mediation might be a requirement that if mediation fails, all issues originally submitted to mediation be referred to fact-finding, regardless of whether tentative agreement had been reached on any portion thereof in mediation. With the hundreds of items often proposed by the parties in the average public sector impasse the horrendous and costly prospect of submitting all items might be enough to stimulate settlement on those few which are still unresolved.

Finally, a requirement that negotiators in mediation be empowered to bind their respective parties would constitute a stimulus to mediated settlement, particularly in view of the increasingly frequent instances of tentative settlements, acceptable to the negotiators themselves, being turned down by organization membership thus triggering the appeal to fact-finding. Similar grants of power might be extended to employer negotiators, at least for noneconomic issues. With a wage freeze in effect, this would have increased feasability.

The foregoing proposals might help to stimulate effective mediation and thus limit appeals to fact-finding. This is the objective. Fact-finding should be preserved for those disputes where every possible effort was made to settle at mediation. There would still be many situations in which fact-finding remains an essential tool for resolving the impasse.

ADJUDICATION OR SETTLEMENT?

It should be noted that fact-finding is not an easily described, or uniform procedure. It is almost universally coupled with the provision of recommendations to the parties for resolving their dispute. These recommendations not being binding on the parties, the process of fact-finding, which is a misnomer itself, is sometimes given another misnomer—advisory arbitration. A greater confusion in the use of the process arises from the role that the fact-finder establishes for himself. Should he be an adjudicator or a mediator? There is one school which insists that the adjudicatory function is required, since mediation has already occurred, and the parties should come to learn that the mediation step rather than the fact-finding step is the proper site for mediated settlement. This, it is argued, would stimulate more sincere mediatory efforts; reduce the tendency to hold back on offers of settlement at earlier steps; and hopefully jolt the parties into recognizing that the most workable solutions, if not achieved in mediation, might readily escape them altogether if the matter is submitted to fact-finding.

The other school of thought holds that the fact-finders should be available to render whatever services are necessary to resolve the parties' impasse, whether it be through mediation or adjudication. Although the adjudicatory approach may be realistic for jurisdictions such as the state of Michigan where the mediators are highly competent, the experience in many other jurisdictions, where staff mediators are more likely to be overworked, inexperienced or even incompetent, dictates that fact-finders should attempt to settle rather than adhere solely to the adjudicatory role. It is true that this tends to dilute the impact of the mediation step, giving two bites at the apple, so to speak, but it also recognizes the greater effectiveness of a mediator with muscle, i.e., the fact-finder who can mediate with the club of a fact-finder's report, possibly adverse, held behind his back. It also permits the fact-finder to assess the range of difference between the parties, and hopefully find an overlapping range of expectations, so that his report can narrow the area of difference and thus be more likely of acceptance by the parties. In this light fact-finding is merely a continuation of the mediating process. As noted in a 1970 report of the Twentieth Century Fund Task Force on Labor Disputes in Public Employment:

> Once the sifting and winnowing have disclosed the true facts to the panel's satisfaction—as opposed to what the parties may have alleged during ne- gotiations—the fact-finders will frequently essay a mediatory role. They will disabuse one or the other or both parties of false notions or assertions, and try to get the parties to agree on settlement terms. In many instances the fact-finding process has succeeded at this point in bringing the dispu- tants into agreement and this has completed its work.

There are those who argue that the fact-finder must disqualify him- self if he accepts the confidences of the parties in a mediatory effort. It would be simple to give either party the option of disqualifying him if confidences gained in mediating are considered to jeopardize his objec- tivity in the fact-finding function.

Just vs. *Acceptable Recommendations*—There are those who argue that the priority of the fact-finder should be a just recommendation rather than an acceptable one. Assuming "just" to be determinable, and assuming the mantle of community responsibility which that label im- plies, it is clear that the responsibility given to the fact-finder by the community is the resolution of employer-employee disputes through the parties' acceptance of his recommendation. The fact-finder has no mandatory power of ordering compliance with his award. That is a function of binding arbitration. Rather, the fact-finder's only tool is a recommendation which he hopes both sides will accept. The parties, rather than the fact-finder, have the community responsibility. They share it. If both agree to a settlement, it must be concluded that com- munity responsibility has been met. If either side, particularly the employer, feels that the community responsibility will be prostituted by submission to an objectionable settlement, then it is duty-bound to reject it and prepare for the consequences. Additionally, ad hoc fact-finders are as susceptible as most to ego satisfaction. The achieve- ment of a mediated settlement, even when hired as a fact-finder, is hard to pass up, even though the long-run relationships between employers and employee organizations might be improved by strict adherence to the rule of no mediating by the fact-finder. Unless so ordered by the designating agencies or specifically prohibited in legislation it is likely that fact-finders will continue their pragmatc approach of "psyching out" a settlement by mediation or by recommendations, the acceptabil- ity of which they have endeavored to ascertain in advance from the parties.

In the foregoing context, the fact-finder's report may mask an understanding reached between the negotiators which they are unable, or perhaps even fearful of trying to sell to their principals. In such a situation the fact-finder's report has an element of objectivity as well as finality attached to it which could increase acceptability of a settlement package.

Aside from such uses (or abuses) of fact-finding it can and does often serve a legitimate function when the mediation step has failed, or even when the fact-finder's mediation effort has been stymied. In such cases the alternatives of either the strike, or total capitulation of one party to the other, may be avoided by a neutral taking a more dispassionate view of the impasse, and making recommendations for settlement.

A fact-finder's report might also prove essential where the public has become embroiled in a dispute over fear of increased taxes, or injustice done to a group of employees. In such a situation the explanation set forth by the fact-finder as to why the settlement should be as recommended can do much to educate and to assuage the community's ire.

This raises the question of whether the fact-finder should limit his role to determination of an equitable level of compensation; or whether he is obligated to go beyond establishment of that objective standard and deal with the employer's ability to pay; or further, set forth a proposal for obtaining the funds to finance what he believes to be a just settlement. There are those who would argue that the fact-finder's role should be the initial, more narrow one of merely proposing appropriate salaries and working conditions. But such tasks cannot be carried out in a vacuum. The employer is almost certainly going to plead inability to pay, and if he does not, the employee organization is guaranteed to point out, in the course of proceedings, that the community has the ability to pay. If this charge is not refuted by the employer it is bound to influence the fact-finder, if only to relieve him of the fear that his recommendations might bankrupt the community.

But regardless of the impact of the parties' arguments relative to ability to pay, I would suggest that the neutral is obligated to consider whether his recommendations can, or ever will, be paid for. This is so for two reasons. First, his proposals for resolution of a problem are advisory and must be in the range of the parties' expectations to be accepted. Indeed, an argument might be made that the more powerful obligation is to "psych-out" the employer; to reach, at least, the fringe of his range of expectations since the employer has the ultimate authority to fund. The second reason for considering ability or inability to pay is that the neutral is called upon to resolve a dispute between two forces in the community. To an extent, even if not designated by a state agency, he bears a public responsibility which, even most narrowly, is to end a dispute; or most widely, to represent the community's interests. In either role his recommendations must be realistic enough to solve the conflict, i.e., propose a tenable, affordable economic settlement. Otherwise, he adds to the conflict rather than resolves it.

The neutral should also recognize that the determination he makes in a particular dispute is likely to have an impact upon other negotiations, other employees, organized as well as unorganized, and even upon the salaries of supervisory personnel, whose salaries are often tied to those in the bargaining unit. He should also consider the impact of an expanded compensation package upon the various programs and priorities of the employer, and his other responsibilities to the community beyond the wage area. And finally, if he has found appropriate a salary schedule beyond current funds, he should recommend to the parties, and the public, the method for attaining its implementation from available or obtainable funds. This is necessary to continue the neutral's credibility, and to increase the likelihood of his proposals being accepted and implemented. Such information should be supplied by the employee organization in support of its argument that there is ability to pay.

IMPROVEMENTS IN FACT-FINDING

When used, the effectiveness of fact-finding might be enhanced in several ways. First, it should be firmly established as the final step in the impasse resolution procedure. The tendency for parties to escalate to mediation because it is available, and then to fact-finding because *it* is available has now taken on a new dimension with either or both of the parties seeking what now is sufficiently common to have an accepted appellation—"superconciliation." As this level of appeal comes to be an accepted part of the machinery, there will be fewer and fewer settlements at the mediation level or even at the level of fact-finding itself. Since the fact-finder's recommendations are bound to stimulate direct discussion between the parties, there is much to be said for placing the fact-finding step before mediation. This might be more realistic and effective since the fact-finder's report, as noted earlier, is not self-initiating and must still be the basis of negotiations between the parties. This is akin to what has happened to collective bargaining in the railroad industry with the real efforts at settlement being made after the fact-finding reports of the presidential emergency boards. But as things stand now, with fact-finding generally the final formal step, making available further steps tends to minimize the value of the earlier steps and propels all realistic dispute settlement to that final step. Thus, a strict hands-off policy following the issuance of the fact-finder's report would do much to stimulate settlement—either during the formal mediation or at the outset of the fact-finding procedure, and most importantly, by the parties themselves in direct negotiations over implementation of the fact-finder's report.

Second, as noted above, fact-finding should be funded by the parties themselves. The argument is made that this places smaller units of government or employees in an adverse position in terms of their inability to pay the fact-finders' services and expenses. This same argument was once raised in the private sector regarding the pressures upon small parties being required to pay for arbitration of grievances. But the evidence indicates that small units still process their grievances to arbitration. The same should be true for fact-finding of new contract terms, with the parties, regardless of size, picking up their share of the cost. The fact that size and limited finances hit equally at small employers as well as the small bargaining unit should provide an additional stimulus to such parties to settle. To have the facility available without cost to the parties would clearly be a stimulus to its use. If, on the other hand, the parties were required to pay for this procedure it would at least lead to a balancing of equities between what had been offered and the cost and uncertainty of going to the next step.

Third, fact-finding as mediation must be carried on outside the pressures of budget deadlines, and the like. It is to the parties' mutual benefit that the fact-finder be assured of ample time to hear the case and write his award without the exertion of undue time pressures by either party.

Fourth, fact-finders should be given discretion as to the publication of their awards. Some legislation requires publication, others leave it up to the discretion of the fact-finder, the parties, or the designating agencies. Likelihood of settlement following a fact-finder's report is greater if the parties are given adequate opportunity for private discussion and perhaps even trade-off of the items therein. To force early publication merely tends to freeze the proposals made by the fact-finder, making it difficult for the parties to use such recommendations as a basis for attaining a more palatable settlement.

Finally, consideration should be given to combining the mediation and fact-finding steps in one person in order to eliminate duplication, thus giving the mediator the greater muscle of being statutorily authorized to make recommendations if his mediation is unsuccessful.

Compulsory Arbitration

The experience of dispute settlement machinery to date has been predominantly in the area of mediation and fact-finding. These steps have been utilized extensively and it must be concluded that they have had their impact in stimulating settlements. Through their establishment many potential strikes on wages, hours, and working conditions have undoubtedly been avoided.

But the strike problem remains and continues to intensify. The procedures of mediation and fact-finding are not universally accepted as final, and strikes continue to be called by employees or forced by employers. This has opened the door to compulsory arbitration as the potential answer. The essential question in considering arbitration of new contract terms is "Will it work?"

Binding arbitration incorporates many of the virtues attributed to fact-finding: 1) the expert neutral; 2) taking evidence from both sides on the merits of their positions in a judicial manner; 3) issuing a report based on what the arbitrator determines to be the appropriate resolution of the dispute. The prime difference of course is that the arbitrator's award is final and binding. This, the advocates of arbitration assert, is what is necessary to bring a finality to employer-employee disputes, to protect the public interest, and to assure that the neutral's report is accepted. It is at the same time the device to bring into line the militant employee groups, as well as the reluctant "king can do no wrong" employers.

The critics of binding arbitration argue that it runs contrary to the traditional concepts of voluntarism inherent in our national labor policy; and that it will deter negotiations or mediation, since the parties will adhere to their extreme positions in the hope that the more extreme their position, the closer to their real goals will come the split-the-difference award. Another objection is the lack of evidence of its workability. A few states have enacted such legislation with, it could be argued, generally favorable results, since the awards have generally been acceptable. The big test arises when the unfavorable binding awards are issued. The evidence of disregard for law by engaging in illegal strikes has been known to occur in the event of unfavorable arbitration awards. The Montreal police strike was called to protest an arbitrator's final award.

It should be emphasized that the objections of many to arbitration of new contract terms does not run to arbitration of grievances. The latter is held acceptable primarily because it arises from a binding arrangement entered into voluntarily with the parties for the life of the agreement.

The problem with the requirement of final and binding arbitration of new contract terms is its compulsory rather than voluntary nature. Certainly voluntary arbitration is not objected to if the parties decide on it and voluntarily agree to be bound by the arbitrator's decision. Rather it is compulsory arbitration that has elicited the negative response by those involved in the labor-management field.

Nonetheless, the rising incidence of strikes and the frustration of seeking settlement through mediation and/or fact-finding virtually forces one to the conclusion that there may indeed be room for arbitration. Maybe *it* is the true substitute for the strike. This may indeed be true for employees engaged in the essential "industries" of police, fire, and perhaps even sanitation. Work stoppages in those fields obviously can paralyze a community, and this realization could lead unscrupulous local organizations to potential "blackmail" because of the inelasticity of the market. At the same time employers are aware of the public wrath that would descend on them if they let such a strike occur and upon the employees in these fields if they took part in such a strike. Both sides now tend to use these threats of public reaction to the strike as their own form of blackmail in the current exercises of brinkmanship which often characterize collective bargaining in these three municipal services. But arbitration, even though compulsory, must maintain the objectivity of judgment and immunity from local pressure that is the keystone of the acceptance of its outcome. In this respect it is noteworthy that the new statute for binding arbitration of police and fire disputes in South Dakota requires that the neutral chairman of the tripartite board be a registered voter of the community involved and that the board's decision be published in at least one local newspaper.

The International Association of Fire Fighters and some police organizations, recognizing that engaging in collective bargaining might force them to strike to enforce their demands, and fearful of the public unacceptability of fire fighters' strikes, have endorsed binding arbitration in the belief that it would achieve employer acceptance of reasonable wage settlements without the public wrath.

Whether binding arbitration will ultimately prove to be the panacea remains to be seen. Maine, Michigan, Pennsylvania, Rhode Island, and Wyoming now provide it for disputes involving police, fire fighters, and certain other public employees; Canada offers it to federal and certain provincial employees; George Meany has suggested its use in the public sector; and in 1971 it was under legislative consideration in New York City. Despite its reported failures in Canada and Michigan, arbitration may nonetheless be the most effective substitute for the strike weapon to resolve disputes in the public sector.

INNOVATIONS IN BINDING ARBITRATION

Other variations of binding arbitration have been suggested as the route to public sector dispute settlement.

In Oklahoma, the police-fire award is binding only if the employer accepts it. A similar proposal is for a show-cause hearing as to why a neutral's findings should not be adopted by both sides. Under this procedure the presumption is that the award is proper and should be accepted by both sides, placing the public burden for voiding the award upon the party which declines to accept it. The alternative to sustaining the award could be a required return to collective bargaining, or freedom to strike.

Under the new Hawaiian statute, binding arbitration is available to the parties if they so select after mediation and fact-finding steps have been concluded.

Another approach which has some popularity is to limit the arbitrator to the full endorsement of either party's last offer. Although this would appear to stimulate the parties to set forth their true final demands, it need not in fact elicit such honesty. Each side is bound to frame its last offer in the light of what it believes will be forthcoming from the other side. And indeed, the "last offers" from both might be little different from their initial positions, placing the arbitrator in an untenable position if he wishes to issue an award which is most likely to provide the greatest assurance of the parties continuing in a good ongoing relationship. Additionally, the number of issues which traditionally constitute an impasse make a simple choice of one side's last offer by the arbitrator not only weighty but, more importantly, conducive to destruction rather than improvement in the parties' relationship. Such an approach might more easily work if the choice were between positions presented on one issue, but too few impasses are so simple.

Other Dispute Settlement Proposals

It has also been suggested that the parties themselves negotiate procedures for assuring comparability of wages and conditions of public sector employees to their private sector counterparts, using a standard of comparison based upon bench-mark jobs and a job evaluation system which assures that public sector employees receive the wage scales arrived at in the private sector collective bargaining process. Binding arbitration could then be established as the device for resolving disputes over intra- or intersector inequities.

One of the most promising of innovations is that raised initially for handling private sector disputes, referred to as the arsenal of weapons approach. This approach would appear to be equally applicable to public sector disputes. Under it the parties who were unable to resolve their impasse by a fixed date would then be confronted with uncertainty as to the next step. They might be given an option, as in the Canadian federal system, of binding arbitration or mediation with an option to strike, or perhaps more effectively be required to follow the course of action dictated by a tripartite or neutral public labor relations board. This board, if so empowered, could order mediation, fact-finding, arbitration, or a combination thereof. It could also, if so authorized, permit the employee organization to strike, or the employer to lock-out, if resumed negotiations proved unsuccessful. The uncertainty as to what "weapons" the impasse could unlock might prove to be a far greater stimulus to meaningful negotiations than would be the ready availability of known machinery.

The innovations continue to flow, and they are to be encouraged for we have not yet found a foolproof means of forestalling or resolving impasses and averting strikes. On the other hand, some favor simple authorization of the strike. New legislation in Hawaii and Pennsylvania permits the strike under certain conditions. In Hawaii employees are free to strike 60 days after the issuance of the fact-finder's report provided a 10-day notice of intent to strike is furnished. The Pennsylvania statute provides for mediation and fact-finding of public sector disputes. It also permits strikes by public employees following completion of mediation and fact-finding.

There is as yet insufficient evidence to ascertain if either of these two states have hit upon "the solution." It is noteworthy, however, that by legalizing the strike after the required procedures are followed, they have not only recognized what had been occurring in any event illegally, but they have forced employees into the dispute settlement procedures as a prerequisite to striking and jolted recalcitrant employers into more realistic bargaining with the awareness that the strike might in fact occur. It could be argued, also, that by making the strike a legal weapon they reduced the likelihood of its use by those employees who, as others elsewhere, had engaged in the strike, even though illegal, to prove that they were not afraid to use it.

The issue of the legality of the strike was considered by the Twentieth Century Fund Task Force, which split in its opinion with one faction adhering to the traditional blanket prohibition of the strike, regardless of essentiality. The other faction acknowledged there should be no strike pending utilization of the appeals procedure but held that:

> . . . equity and fairness require that public employees have the opportunity to strike when the government authority with decision-making power refuses to accept the recommendation for settling a dispute that has been made by fact-finders. It sees no other effective means of protest open to employees who may feel victimized after the publicly promulgated recommendations of fact-finders have failed to engender pressures sufficient to secure employer acceptance. But even this limited opportunity for a legally acceptable strike would be further restrained either by statutory enactment or by common law, on the theory that public health and safety remain paramount . . .

Conclusion

In reviewing various procedures and possibilities I come back to the view that most likely the ideal solution will rest with the parties learning to negotiate with each other in good faith and with mutual respect. In the long run, as in the short, the only effective dispute settlement procedure is voluntary settlement by the parties themselves.

A. H. Raskin

9

Politics Up-Ends the Bargaining Table

Changing Character of Problem

"The best politics is good government," said Alfred E. Smith when he was governor of New York State nearly a half-century ago. Fiorello H. La Guardia had a slightly different way of putting it when he was mayor of New York City a decade later. "There is no Democratic or Republican method of collecting garbage or regulating traffic," was the Little Flower's formulation.

But the multiplicity of similar strictures by the patron saints of both parties has never masked the reality that mayors and governors—even presidents—must be conscious of politics if they and their policies are to prevail. One expression of that consciousness, especially in the big cities, always has been a strong admixture of politics in the public service—a factor that has grown in insidiousness with the mushrooming of the municipal bureaucracy and of municipal payrolls.

True, the character of the problem has changed drastically. The crudities of the old boodle gangs, which used public jobs as cement for the whole structure of political bossism, have largely disappeared. But the emergence of strongly entrenched unions in control of essential services has created new pressures of such intensity that New York's Mayor John V. Lindsay did not exaggerate when he warned that "the plight of the cities is on the bargaining table." The extent to which politics has helped shape these changes in the civic power balance and now is itself being reshaped by them requires appraisal as part of any balanced assessment of collective bargaining in the public sector.

From the heyday of the Tweed Ring and Tammany Hall a century ago, the Curleys, the Hagues, the Crumps, and the Prendergasts built

A. H. RASKIN, *assistant editor of the editorial page of* The New York Times, *is one of the nation's best known commentators on labor matters.*

their machines on the fealty of city and county employees. Municipal jobs were a payoff for political allegiance—votes, campaign manpower, ballot stuffing, cash kickbacks to the party overlords. And jobs also became the instrument for integrating into the community (as staunch supporters of the machine) the successive waves of immigrants that poured into the cities. Their potential for disruption was defused by giving them a stake in public service: the Irish in police, fire and transit, the Italians in sanitation and public works, the Jews in the school system—but only after an uphill fight with the dominant Catholics.

Changing urban patterns eventually eroded that system of control in most places, a change hastened by the passage at the end of the last century of state civil service reform laws designed to make merit, rather than politics, the basis for appointments and promotions. New York State led the way in 1883 with a law intended to banish the spoilsmen; Massachusetts followed a year later, but by 1910 only four other states had joined the slow-moving parade.

One reason for this slowness was that the spoils system did not vanish merely because the law told it to drop dead, any more than strikes disappear at the drop of a legislative mandate these days. Complaints of evasion of the rules requiring competitive examinations and prohibiting political assessments were widespread. In fact, it was widely charged in the early reform years that the main purpose of many administrators was to find ways to circumvent the rules and operate under politics as usual.

Even today, with the big-city machines in an advanced state of decay, some conspicuous exceptions flourish, principally because their base among public employees remains strong. The mayor of Philadelphia, James H. J. Tate, owed his reelection in 1967 primarily to the activities of unionized civil service employees and their allies in organized labor.

The coalition that has enabled Mayor Richard Daley to turn Chicago into a duchy extends far beyond municipal labor. Yet the artfulness with which Daley manipulates his public employees has brought a spontaneous tribute from the mayor of neighboring Gary, Indiana, Richard Hatcher. "However well or poorly Mayor Daley may use his authority," says Hatcher, "the actions of America's last great political machine in Chicago demonstrate convincingly that patronage politics provides a way to get things done."

Unionization has not undermined Daley's influence over civil service employees. If anything, his bonds to the union leaders have heightened that influence. Even their battles with the Daley administration are sham battles, quickly settled on terms that bring little unhappiness to City Hall.

New York City Situation

In New York City the picture is quite different. It bears detailed exploration, not solely because New York City dwarfs all other American cities in size but also because its problems are even more elephantine. Every affliction that goes into the urban crisis asserts itself most virulently in New York, and none is currently more troublesome than the relationship between the city and its organized employees—some 300,000 out of the 380,000 on the civic payroll. The city's annual outlay on wages, pensions, and other employee benefits grew from $3 billion to $5 billion from 1968 to 1971—years of steady downhill slide in the quality of municipal services. The 1971 payroll figure came to $625 a year in cost for every man, woman, and child in the five boroughs. But since 1.2 million of the 8 million population were on welfare, that figure considerably understates the true expense to each taxpayer of keeping civil service employees in the style to which they were becoming accustomed.

It is arguable perhaps that no amount of pay is adequate to compensate New York City employees for the daily tortures that are inescapable in their jobs. All the fears, frustrations, and furies of the city beat down on them. The policeman, once a symbol of authority, finds himself dodging sniper's bullets or being spat upon as a pig. The fireman, responding to alarms in the ghetto, is peppered with bricks and bottles as he prepares to risk his life to save someone else's. The teacher, already dismayed by the bars to learning created by poverty, family breakup and the general hopelessness of inherited dependency, must also wrestle with the new tensions born of the Negro's struggle for more self-rule. In every other phase of municipal service, the woes of the metropolis make each day's duties a challenge—and usually a misery—for those who work for the city. With these irritations goes an upsurge in living costs that continually outpaces the steep rise everywhere else—or did until President Nixon instituted his wage-price freeze in August 1971.

Disagreeable as all these pressures are, they leave many New Yorkers unpersuaded that the community is getting anything like the return it should for its gargantuan investment in better wages and other protections for city employees. This public discontent with both the quantity and quality of municipal services is by no means confined to the rich and middle-income families, who pay the great bulk of the taxes. On the contrary, the most explosive complaints come from the slum districts, constantly on the lip of revolt over inadequate garbage collections, dilapidated public housing, police abuses, or a thousand other types of civic neglect. The result is a kind of low-voltage guerrilla warfare between slumdwellers and their supposed friends and protectors in the civil service, a warfare that often erupts in violence and occasionally in riot.

The odd thing about New York's experience is that no city embraced more quickly or more thoroughly that touchstone of sound municipal labor-management relations, hallowed in every manual of orderly governmental personnel practice: the notion that public employees should not be treated as second-class citizens, expected to subsidize the city by working for substandard wages and denied machinery for the democratic adjustment of grievances through representatives of their own choosing.

As far back as 1958 Mayor Robert F. Wagner, Jr., had promulgated a comprehensive code for union recognition and collective bargaining within the framework of civil service laws and regulations. The New York plan was evolved by Ida Klaus, then counsel to the city Labor Department, after the most definitive study in any community of how employer-employee relations in the public service could be conducted most fruitfully.

Her conclusion was that the city's business would be run with maximum efficiency if machinery were provided for collective bargaining. "Human nature is such that paternalism, no matter how bounteous its gifts, may be of less real satisfaction and advantage to both sides than the process of reasoning together around the family table, no matter how meager the fare," Miss Klaus told the mayor. A similar belief that, through union representation, standards of service to the public will go up along with standards of equity for those who serve the public remains the foundation for the increasing adoption all over the country of systems comparable to those institutionalized by New York's pioneering code. It is precisely that belief which New York's experience brings most into question, largely because it has proved impossible to keep power politics out of the equation.

O'Dwyer-Wagner Cooperation with Unions

Actually, the 1958 program merely put into citywide context practices already long established in many parts of the municipal service, with the city-owned subways and bus lines as the prime example. It all began when William O'Dwyer recaptured City Hall for the Democrats in 1945 after twelve years of Fusion rule under La Guardia. The new mayor's first encounter with the Transport Workers Union (TWU) and its bellicose but wily president, Michael J. Quill, was unpromising. Reports that the Board of Transportation planned to turn the subway system's independent power houses over to private operation by Consolidated Edison brought a strike threat from Quill, who made up in lung power what his union then lacked in strength. O'Dwyer disavowed the transfer plan under circumstances that evoked charges of "appeasement" from editorial writers and business leaders. So upset was the mayor by his apparent loss of face that he began confiding to every City Hall visitor that the town was not big enough to hold him and Mike Quill and that he would cut the TWU leader down to size the next time they tangled.

An opportunity came almost at once. The union asked for higher wages and sole bargaining rights for all transit employees. By way of proving that he could be tough when the situation demanded, O'Dwyer refused to let Quill into his office when the final settlement was being signed with the aid of Philip Murray, national president of the Congress of Industrial Organizations. Chief item in the pact was appointment of a committee to decide how big an increase the workers should get and, far more important in long-range terms, how inclusive the new bargaining mechanism should be. When the committee's report came, it went so far toward satisfying the union that one jubilant Quill aide crowed: "We not only brought home the bacon, we brought home the whole pig."

That was the start of a beautiful friendship, which achieved full ripeness in 1948 when O'Dwyer gave the transit workers a fat pay boost and Quill cheerfully became the political fall guy for doubling the nickel subway fare, a sacred cow that was fast eating up the whole city treasury.

The relationship between City Hall and the civil service unions got chummier still after Wagner—the son of the author of labor's Magna Carta, the Wagner Act—came in as mayor in 1954. Strike threats were frequent, but strikes were few. In general, unions found that a show of muscle resulted in getting the city to cough up money it said it did not have. The idea spread that militancy paid off—if only because it provided an excuse City Hall felt it needed to convince the taxpayers that it was not throwing New York's money away.

Again the TWU provided the light at the end of the subway tunnel, trailblazing on a track that had more to do with politics than orthodox collective bargaining. Quill, a showman on a par with Jimmy Cagney or John Wayne, put on a great exhibition of bellicosity in every negotiation. All the conventional trappings were there—a mammoth rank-and-file negotiating committee, distinguished mediators to assist in the climactic phases—but when it came to the clutch Quill and Wagner would meet in total privacy to hammer out a settlement. Eureka, the trains would run.

Behind the hippodroming was a sustained exercise in palmanship that carried explicit dividends for both mayor and union leader. The contracts, for all the flamboyance of Quill's victory claims, were always well within the range of reason. And the TWU, after the television cameras had been turned off, was a model of cooperation in raising standards of operating efficiency by permitting the squeeze-out of thousands of jobs in the deficit-ridden system. Indeed, this cooperation extended to such lengths that the transit system fell into a perilous state of undermanning.

MAKING THE TWU DOMINANT

The city, for its part, did everything in its power to make Quill and his union feel secure. One specific thing it could and did do was to help the TWU chief smash the dissidence of splinter unions representing motormen, conductors, towermen, bus maintainers, and other skilled crafts. In fairness, there were discernible advantages for the city in having a single union speak for all the 30,000 employees of the mass transportation lines, chief among them the reduced danger of whipsawing on wages, interunion raids, and quickie strikes messing up the interdependent system. Conversely, there was the risk that the deliberate herding of all workers into one union would give it total power over the city's transportation lifeline, putting all New Yorkers at its mercy whenever it chose to strike.

In December 1957, the long-festering anger of the craftsmen at the city's partisanship for the TWU exploded in an eight-day strike of motormen, backed by seven other crafts. The specific irritant was the fixing by the Transit Authority of a date for a systemwide election intended to give the TWU exclusive representation rights over all divisions and thus banish the last vestiges of splinter unionism.

The walkout caused substantial disruption of transportation, despite the most energetic joint endeavors by the city and the union to break it. No hirer of Pearl Bergoff or the Pinkertons in the prime of the "American plan" used more dirty tricks to thwart a strike than did the TWU-Transit Authority alliance. Strike leaders were sent to jail, bonuses paid to nonstrikers, mass reprisals threatened against the strikers, all with the encouragement of the dominant union. The final straw came with the planting of labor spies at meetings of the Motormen's Benevolent Association and the "bugging" of its headquarters. When discovery of a hidden microphone brought these Big Brother methods to public notice, Mayor Wagner thundered: "Whoever is responsible for the bugging is going to regret it, mark my words. I'm mad as hell." The evidence was unmistakable that both the Transit Authority and the police were up to their eardrums in the electronic eavesdroppers, but nothing ever came of the disciplinary threat.

The strike ended on the basis of a promise by the Republicans in control of the State Legislature to mandate provisions for craft separation along the lines prescribed for private industry by the Taft-Hartley Act. Nothing ever came of that promise either. Instead, the systemwide election went off, as scheduled, and the TWU scored a decidedly unimpressive "victory." More than half of the 30,000 workers boycotted the balloting in response to a stayaway campaign fostered by the dissident crafts. The Quill union was certified with only 10,000 votes, as against the 25,000 it had received in a somewhat similar poll three years earlier.

The result was doubly indicative of the TWU's weakness because Quill, in urging a large turnout, had linked the size of the pay increase the union could expect to win in forthcoming negotiations with the city to the size of its election plurality. "The bigger the vote, the bigger the increase," was the union's campaign slogan.

In the contract talks, which reached the showdown stage only a few days after the motormen called off their insurrection, Quill dropped the mantle of public protector he had worn so righteously throughout the earlier tie-up and returned to his more familiar role of werewolf of the underground. When Wagner, faithful to his part in the time-worn scenario, warned that the city would not tolerate a strike, Quill denounced him as "a second-rate Coolidge." To no one's vast surprise, peace came a few hours before the New Year's Eve deadline on terms favorable enough to give Quill a running start toward reknitting the fragmented ranks of his union. Included was an inequity adjustment fund to help woo back the disgruntled craftsmen. The motormen now have a special status inside the union that keeps them on the reservation.

It would be an exaggeration to pretend that the political interplay between the Quill-led TWU and the Wagner administration was typical of the relationship everywhere in the civil service. Quill was a unique type and so was the operating method he devised. But other civil service unions grew swiftly in strength and security under the policies of a mayor who lost no opportunity to proclaim that New York was a "union town."

Working Through the Labor Leaders

The key conduit outside of transit was Harry Van Arsdale, Jr., the tireless president of the Central Labor Council. He was the man to see when a union wanted action by the city, whether it involved a member's wife in quick need of admission to a municipal hospital or a commissioner's ruling that could jeopardize a thousand jobs. The niceties of union protocol got as much attention in Wagner's dealings with Van Arsdale as diplomatic protocol gets in U Thant's dealings with President Nixon or Premier Kosygin. Wagner's invariable question when his chief labor adviser, Theodore W. Kheel, came to him with a proposal affecting labor was, "Have you cleared this with Van Arsdale?" The only exception was transit. Then the question became, "Have you cleared this with Quill?" The result was that the union establishment was never caught off base by a Wagner move.

On top of all that, Wagner was always at pains to give the union hierarchy a feeling of importance, even if he did not give their members as much money as they wanted at contract time. No union function was official without a visit from the mayor. The duty round did not stop with conventions, testimonial dinners, luncheons, funerals, weddings, and installations of officers. It ran right through the weekend to unveilings, confirmations, and bar mitzvahs for sons, daughters, nephews, nieces, and even grandchildren.

Lindsay and the Unions

Things changed noticeably when Republican John Lindsay came in as a reform mayor in 1966. Even before he got to City Hall, Lindsay let it be known that the highly politicized bargaining structure was high up on the list of things he intended to reform. He inveighed against "power brokers"—a term everyone promptly translated to read Van Arsdale and Kheel—and announced his resolve to get more science into negotiations by using impartial fact-finders to make recommendations when deadlocks developed.

1966 TRANSIT STRIKE DISASTER

The first test of this brave resolution almost proved lethal—for the city. The subways and buses started a twelve-day sleep five hours after Lindsay took the oath of office. Every aspect of the negotiations was a disaster, with the new mayor outmaneuvered throughout by the crafty Quill. Part of the problem was that the contract talks started under Wagner and wound up under Lindsay, with neither having either love or trust for the other.

Picking mediators to get everybody across the trestle without a train-wreck proved a monumental task. Quill made it plain that he would never agree to any peacemaking panel unless Kheel were a member. He got his way on that. He won again in objecting to permitting the mediators to make settlement recommendations, part of the Lindsay concept—a concept with plenty of precedents in the Wagner era. Quill dug in so adamantly against fact-finding that Nathan W. Feinsinger, chairman of the panel, informed Lindsay that he would pack his bag and go back to Wisconsin if the mayor insisted on recommendations.

In hindsight, most observers were convinced that Quill needed so big a wage increase in 1966 that no mayor could have given it without a strike. Negroes and Puerto Ricans, starting from jobs at the bottom of the wage ladder, were becoming an increasingly substantial part of the TWU rank and file, and the Irish leadership would have felt obliged to prove its effectiveness by delivering a whopping pay raise even if Wagner had still been top banana at City Hall.

However, there was no doubt that Quill took extra delight in humiliating "Lindsley," the elegant Yalie who had made so manifest his disdain for all the Quill bag of tricks. The TWU chief was near death from heart disease; he had to swallow great gobs of pills in his moments of privacy; but none of this dulled his appetite for melodrama. He went before the television cameras to tear up no-strike injunctions like confetti. When a judge ordered him carted off to jail, he said, "Let the judge drop dead in his black robes." A heart seizure forced Quill's own transfer to the prison ward at Bellevue Hospital. But when a delegation from the Central Labor Council sought to have him released, it developed that Quill preferred his martyrdom. The union missionaries, headed by Van Arsdale, made their initial plea to Lindsay. He assured them that he had no wish to see any unionist in jail and advised them to put their request before Joseph E. O'Grady, chairman of the Transit Authority, which had officially initiated the contempt move that resulted in Quill's incarceration.

O'Grady, a carryover from the Wagner period and an old hand at dealing with the TWU president, gave the Central Labor Council representatives a quizzical look when they made their bid for Quill's freedom. "Have you asked the union whether they want him out?" was his somewhat disconcerting question. The puzzled delegation sought out Douglas MacMahon, the TWU chief of staff in Quill's enforced absence. "Why don't you guys mind your own business?" was all he had to say. That ended the effort to get Quill sprung; it was too obvious that he relished standing alongside Eugene V. Debs and other labor heroes imprisoned for their dedication to the workingman. More important, he was confident that the combined impact of public clamor for swift restoration of subway service and sympathy for his plight could be parlayed into extra "milluns" for his members. The cost of the two-year contract negotiated with a nod from his hospital bed was double that of any previous transit labor accord.

AMELIORATION

The next two years brought many reverses, few successes, in Lindsay's relations with civil service unions. Then came a dramatic turnaround in the place where the mayor had flubbed most badly—transit. His conduct in the 1968 TWU negotiations earned him high praise from the man who took Quill's place, Matthew Guinan, a unionist much less given to histrionics but no less resolute in negotiations. Old Wagner aides joined in the cheers. "The difference between the Lindsay of 1966 and the Lindsay of 1968 was like night and day," said Kheel, whose manipulative talents and resourcefulness had restored him to almost as prominent a troubleshooting role in the new administration as he had had in the old.

The thing most of the applauders liked best was that Lindsay had not insisted on fact-finding. He had left it to the union and the

Transit Authority, aided by the old pros, to work out their own settlement. They did it without a strike, but the price went up—a circumstance that did not differentiate it from agreements being signed in private or public employment everywhere else. In relations with other unions as he began his third year, the mayor was plainly trying hard to get away from the "holier than thou" pose labor had found so exasperating in earlier months. He acquired at least a little of the concern Wagner had shown for shoring up the internal prestige of local union leaders and making them look good in the eyes of their membership. And he carried forward the notion of trying to make unions responsible by making them strong. An embracing unit was established to lump 120,000 clerical, administrative, and maintenance workers—almost everybody outside the uniformed services, schools, and transit—in a catch-all bargaining pool for pensions and a variety of other issues. District Council 37 of the American Federation of State, County and Municipal Employees (AFSCME), AFL-CIO, skyrocketed in dues payments under the new arrangement. In the Wagner period the council, under the leadership of Jerry Wurf, a hard-driving loner, had stood outside the "club" that maintained a cozy palship with City Hall. But, when Wurf went to Washington shortly before the shift in mayors to head the fast-growing parent union, his successor, Victor Gotbaum, moved into a political and operational alliance with Lindsay almost as pervasive as the one Van Arsdale and Quill had previously had with Wagner.

CHANGES IN LEGAL FRAMEWORK

While these changes in attitude and power lineup were taking form at City Hall, significant changes were also occurring in the legal framework affecting collective bargaining and strikes in the civil service. The state's Condon-Wadlin Act prohibiting strikes by municipal and state employees had become a casualty of the 1966 transit strike. Adopted after a Buffalo teachers' strike in 1948, it prescribed strike penalties so draconian no official could enforce them. The lush settlement of the subway stoppage—a patent violation of a Condon-Wadlin prohibition on giving strikers any pay increase for three years—brought a taxpayers' suit to upset the contract.

When a judge agreed that the pact was invalid, the TWU threatened a fresh strike. Van Arsdale speedily invoked his political credit cards at Albany to take both the union and the city off the spot. A lifelong Democrat, the peppery Central Labor Council head had never found it hard to get along with Republicans if they were prepared to be friendly. Governor Nelson A. Rockefeller, whose ties with Van Arsdale matched those between the union chief and Wagner, moved at once to push through the legislature a bill giving retroactive forgiveness to the transit strikers.

With Condon-Wadlin thus defanged, the governor turned to five prestigious experts in labor-management relations headed by Professor George W. Taylor of the Wharton School at the University of Pennsylvania for recommendations on a new law. Its emphasis was on peace prodecures, rather than punishment for individual strikers. I will forbear to discuss its details here since they are covered in other chapters. Suffice it to say that labor lobbyists, irked because it maintained a blanket ban on strikes, did succeed in watering down its penalties against striking unions even though they could not block its passage. Later the New York City civil service unions joined in a massive rally to vow political extermination for all the legislative sponsors of the Taylor Law.

Simultaneously, New York City was enacting a local law of its own designed to establish greater harmony on the public employee front. Its genesis was a project Wagner and the municipal unions had initiated in cooperation with the American Arbitration Association. Out of studies by an association task force came an Office of Collective Bargaining (OCB), underwritten by the city and the unions. Its goal was to prevent strikes by making them unnecessary, but unlike the state law it did not explicitly prohibit strikes if all its elaborate mechanism for third-party intervention failed to effect a meeting of minds. The lack of finality in any of its procedures put the OCB in a kind of twilight zone; the state delegated to it authority to administer all normal aspects of labor relations, including mediation and fact-finding, but the mandatory Taylor Law sanctions came into play if anyone struck. In the jockeying that led to the OCB's establishment, Gotbaum, whose brainpower puts him well ahead of most of his associates in municipal unionism's upper echelon, solidified his position as "No. 1" in the emerging power structure at City Hall. Van Arsdale, for his part, signaled a desire to be correct, if not cordial, in dealings with the mayor by accepting membership in the new agency's top policy board. George Meany hailed the whole set-up as a national model.

1968 SANITATION STRIKE

Just when things seemed headed back toward some chilly approximation of the old amity, the city met Armageddon on a garbage dump. A runaway strike of sanitation employees turned Fun City into a playground for rats and vermin; and five boroughs were buried under 100,000 tons of uncollected refuse. The onslaught of the strike in February 1968 was as much a surprise to the union as it was to the city.

The head of the Uniformed Sanitationmen's Association, John J. DeLury, is a fast-talking, dapper little man, whose organization is more political machine than union. Never encumbered with modesty, he is wont to boast of the union's ability to muster votes for its favored candidates. "Only God can guarantee 100 percent delivery," says DeLury. "We are sure of 99 percent based on past performance." He supported Democrat Abraham D. Beame against Lindsay in the 1965 campaign, then went all-out for Governor Rockefeller's reelection a year later.

In 1968 DeLury was boycotting the OCB but he had no quarrel with pay increases recommended for his union by two mediators appointed by the mayor (one of them Arvid Anderson, chairman of the OCB). The only trouble was that the rank and file hooted the proposal down at what DeLury hoped would be a victory rally, and he found himself obliged to pedal furiously to avoid being deserted by his rebellious army.

As the city sank into an ocean of swill, Lindsay reverted to his pre-election idea that there were limits beyond which the community should not let itself be pushed, no matter how painful the confrontation. He was personally fed up and he sensed that a good part of the citizenry was fed up too. One other thing made him feel he could not trot out the old appeasement routine to coax the sanitationmen back to work. His telephone kept ringing with calls from the heads of other municipal unions warning him that OCB was dead if DeLury's people got more by overriding their leaders and thumbing their nose at the Taylor Law.

When the strike's first week ended with the garbage trucks still in dead storage, the mayor appealed to the governor to call out the National Guard. Instead, Rockefeller took over the role of super-mediator in command of efforts to find a peace formula. The leaders of the citywide labor movement, all buddies of the governor, were called in to offer their advice. It could be summed up: "Give the union a little more. Save DeLury's face and get everybody back on the job."

An expanded mediation panel, created by the governor with Lindsay's unenthusiastic assent, recommended a pay increase just a little better than the one the union members had spurned. Rockefeller pronounced the proposal "fair and reasonable"; the union felt the same way. But an angry Lindsay denounced it as "a little bit of blackmail" and said the city would never pay it. He warned that the plan's acceptance would wreck both respect for law (what little there was of it in municipal unionism) and the delicate balance that kept all the unions in the civil service from climbing over one another's backs in an endless pyramid.

The governor's reply, after an attempt at arbitration broke down, was to announce that he would ask the legislature to approve a temporary state takeover of the city Sanitation Department, with the workers to go back to their jobs at the higher pay recommended by his mediators. The city would have the privilege of paying the bill for this nominal state operation. The union, jubilant at the humiliation thus inflicted on the mayor, sent its members back without waiting for legislative ratification of the Rockefeller plan.

Welcome as New Yorkers found the sight of big yellow trucks gobbling up the avalanche of waste, few had a kind word to say for the cute trick that got the trucks rolling. Suddenly, the mayor didn't look like a stiff-necked, petulant bumbler any more. The people overwhelmingly sided with him in his not-one-penny-for-tribute stand. "Cool Hand Luke," as one union wag labeled him, had snatched the initiative away from the men who thought he had exposed himself as a hopelessly outclassed amateur.

The cowed legislative leaders decided to take everybody in Albany off the spot by putting the governor's takeover plan in the deep freeze. The ball passed back to the mayor, and the city started trying to negotiate where it had left off before the strike. In the end, the job was turned over to an arbitrator for final and binding decision. The man picked for that touchy assignment was Vincent D. McDonnell, chairman of the State Mediation Board, who ranked high with both Lindsay and Rockefeller. By an exercise in fancy footwork worthy of Fred Astaire, he closed out the incident by coming up with an award in which everyone could claim vindication.

The political fallout did not clear for a long time. Lindsay, nurturing long-range aspirations to the White House, got a big boost in national political oomph as a man who had faced down the union bosses. Rockefeller, whose designs on the 1968 Republican Presidential nomination were very specific, found that his buddy-buddy approach to the strike had moved his stock down to the bottom of the garbage can. The municipal unionists, not quick to forgive or forget, licked their wounds. To them the mayor's call for the National Guard had been like waving a bloody shirt, a reminder of labor's ancestral battles, and it galled them to see him come out with a political plus.

1968 TEACHERS' STRIKE

All their irritation found outlet seven months later when the school year opened with a citywide teachers' strike that posed in starkest terms the collision of union and community interests—a collision that over the years is likely to put greater strains on the capacity for survival of all our big cities than the traditional "battle for the buck" in contract negotiations.

The 1968 school strike grew out of a running battle between the United Federation of Teachers (UFT) and groups of militant black and Puerto Rican parents seeking a larger voice in the administration of neighborhood schools. The spark that touched off the strike was the forced transfer of some union teachers out of the Ocean Hill-Brownsville demonstration school district in Brooklyn. The district, embracing a slum so dilapidated it evokes memories of bomb-ravaged cities in World War II, was the scene of an experiment in school decentralization, a test of community control.

The union had all the best of the legal argument on the narrow strike issue. Unquestionably, the teachers were being shifted in violation of contract by parents who had decided they did not want them. But the union's decision to make the entire school system the battleground—a decision in which it enlisted the full support of organized school principals and administrators—caused a rush to the barricades on both sides of a swiftly polarized city.

What was involved had been well summarized months before the tie-up by John Doar, former United States Assistant Attorney General in charge of civil rights enforcement, whom Lindsay had enlisted as president of the central Board of Education. "Union concepts of security and seniority were formulated in the period of struggle between company and union. Now the struggle is between the Negroes and the unions. . . . It is our position that a basic conflict exists between labor union concepts and civil rights concepts. Something has to give."

What seemed in danger of giving as the school strike raged on were the frayed cords that held this tense city together. Premier Golda Meir of Israel, visiting New York during the strike, was so dismayed at the blatant racism she heard on every side that she declared, "This is still a ghettoized community." Relations between Lindsay and the Central Labor Council plummeted to minus-zero. When the mayor sought to mend things by naming Ted Kheel, mainstay of the old Wagner labor team, as chairman of a panel to try to settle the strike, Van Arsdale asserted that there was nothing to mediate and urged Kheel to stay out.

After ten weeks of searing conflict, a combination of universal exhaustion, political manipulation over decentralization at City Hall and in Albany, and racial crosspulls inside the Central Labor Council brought a settlement on terms the city felt both the UFT and the black community could live with. Van Arsdale, who had backed the teachers unreservedly, found the ground being pulled out from under him by mounting dissidence among unions with large black and Puerto Rican membership. Gotbaum's District Council 37 was in the vanguard of the rebellion. Guinan's Transport Workers Union became a surprise added starter, a reflection of the swift rise in its non-white ratio. The divisions which the strike had exacerbated in the larger community had fragmented labor's own traditional strike solidarity.

ME-TOOISM IN UNIFORMED FORCES' NEGOTIATIONS

The paramount conclusion Lindsay derived from the whole rending experience was that the city and its unions had to learn to live together again or there would be no city to live in. What is more, the next mayoral election was now just a year off and it was plain that Lindsay could never hope to mend his creaky coalition if the next negotiations in the city's non-stop bargaining calendar, those involving police, fire and sanitation, wound up in yet another disaster.

By way of insurance against any such dire outcome, the mayor prevailed on Arthur J. Goldberg, then fresh out of his post as United States Ambassador to the United Nations, to head up a super-duper mediation panel to make pay recommendations for integrated contracts covering all three uniformed forces.

The point of the exercise was to end the rash of "me-tooism" that kept the civic payroll climbing as each union flexed its muscles for everything anyone else had gotten, plus a few extra sweeteners for itself. One Lindsay aide noted that the unions had got so skilled at slide-rule mathematics that they could give lessons in precision calculation to the computer wizards at the Manned Space Center in Houston.

The Goldberg panel's formula was to use that familiar solvent, a substantial chunk of the city's money, to get all the uniformed services into one time frame and one pay structure. It involved parity for police and fire and 90 percent parity for sanitation. The executive boards of all three unions endorsed the recommendation, but the police and fire rank and file demanded more. An epidemic of "Hong Kong flu" hit the Police Department; the firemen refused to do anything but answer alarms. The city went back to the old way of handling such disruptions; it retired the panel and bought its way out by tacking more cash onto the fat package originally proposed.

Something else happened at the same time that the public never found out about until much later—too late to do anything but dig deep into the city's near-bankrupt treasury for another big wad of taxpayers' cash. In the clandestine talks that led to the 1969-70 agreement, the city's bargainers had committed it to the ultimate in "me-tooism," an almost incredible postscript to a contract round chiefly designed to padlock the treasury against such interunion leapfrogging.

Background—A bit of backtracking is needed to explain the box the city got itself into. Since 1898 the city had paid the same basic wage to firemen and patrolmen. However, there were fluctuating differentials in the pay scales for the first promtion grades in the two departments—police sergeants and fire lieutenants. In the Wagner administration, the ratios were frozen at a level that established this balance: patrolmen to police sergeants—3 to 3.5; firemen to fire lieutenants—3 to 3.9.

In 1967 the police sergeants, unhappy over the disparity, filed an action with the OCB to establish their right to the same pay as the first promotion grade in fire. A panel, headed by David L. Cole, concluded that the responsibilities of police officers were "certainly not of a lower order" than those of fire officers. It recommended that the city move toward equalizing the two pay scales, but out of consideration for the unsettling effect such a shift would have all up and down the line on other city pay scales the panel suggested that only half the gap be closed right away. That made the ratio 3 to 3.7 in police, as against 3 to 3.9 in fire.

Everybody except the police sergeants and higher-ranking police officers was made unhappy by that award. The fire lieutenants saw no reason why their edge over police sergeants should be narrowed. The patrolmen, for their part, wanted to be brought back up to a 3 to 3.5 balance with the men one grade above them. Goldberg had opened the door for just such an adjustment (without acknowledging explicitly that was what he was doing) by including in his panel's report a $500-a-year payment for "restoration of the differential between patrolmen and sergeants" that existed before the Cole reshuffle.

In the talks that upped the ante still further, the city specifically tied into the new agreement an initialed statement by Herbert L. Haber, its labor relations director, that it was the city's "intent" to preserve the 3 to 3.5 ratio for patrolmen, no matter what salary might ultimately be agreed on for sergeants. Predictably, that commitment led the city into a nutcracker from which it could not extricate itself without excruciating pain.

In November 1969, Kheel, as impasse officer in a new OCB case filed by the sergeants, held that he had no choice except to follow through on the thrust of the initial Cole decision. He ordered a closing of the whole gap between police sergeants and fire lieutenants, thus establishing a 3 to 3.9 ratio for both departments. Effectuation of the Kheel award meant that patrolmen and firemen were on the same level, with salaries of $10,950 a year, and police sergeants and fire lieutenants were 30 percent above them, with annual salaries of $14,235.

The Patrolmen's Benevolent Association (PBA) moved into court to assert its right to a further increase—one that would bring its members up to the 3 to 3.5 ratio prescribed by the secret memorandum. The firemen lost no time in letting it be known that whatever the cops got they would have to get too, and sanitation was right behind with a claim for its 90 percent matching payment. The "me-too" express was swinging into full throttle again. Before it roared to a halt, loaded with goodies for everybody, the PBA members had gone on a five-day wildcat strike and the firefighters harassed the city with job actions.

Political Hostility—The thing that became clearest in the wrangle was the virulence of the political hostility felt by the police and fire unions toward the Lindsay administration. The "Irish Mafia," which had long dominated the Police Department, had been outraged from the start at what they regarded as undue political interference by the mayor in their bailiwick, especially when that interference took the form of protection for black militants, draft protestors, and other rebels.

The animosity surfaced in a November 1966 referendum on a Lindsay-sponsored Civilian Review Board to pass on charges of police brutality. The PBA mounted a successful campaign to persuade the voters that approval of the board would foster lawlessness and make New Yorkers fearful to walk the streets. The combined efforts of the mayor and Senators Robert F. Kennedy and Jacob K. Javits proved pitifully inadequate to counter these appeals to fear and the board died under a cascade of ballots.

The PBA and the mayor were often at swordspoint after that over City Hall's attempts to dilute entrance standards to make it easier for Negroes and Puerto Ricans to get police jobs, over cost-effectiveness studies and official inquiries into police graft, and over Lindsay attempts to utilize manpower more effectively through assignment of one man, instead of two, to prowl cars and through repeal of a 1911 state law mandating a three-platoon system for spreading policemen over 24 hours.

Clashes with the Uniformed Firefighters Association, though less frequent, were equally bitter. The mental set that developed out of these conflicts was one which made the two unions almost phobic in their distrust of the mayor when the negotiations for a 1971 contract ran into heavy going even before the courts had disposed of the parity pay dispute. The acuteness of the hostility was probably best reflected in the way Edward J. Kiernan, president of the PBA, sought to capitalize on it as a means of keeping his members from a second walkout after the mayor had announced his intention of invoking the mandatory Taylor Law penalties against those who had taken part in the initial wildcat. "Do not give this man what he wants—the presidency of the United States, the destruction of the PBA and the ruination of New York City," Kiernan said by way of calming his men. It worked.

So did the court suit for retroactive back pay. A State Supreme Court justice upheld the patrolmen's right to a boost of $1,200 a year to restore the 3 to 3.5 ratio. Along with the raise went retroactivity for the months from October 1968 through December 1970, a tidy lump of $2,700 for each man. The city speedily decided that the only effect of an appeal would be to risk inclusion in the final award of retroactive adjustments covering pensions, overtime, and other allowances as well as base pay. It settled out of court for a $1,200 increase, plus back pay, then gave the same deal to firemen and $120 less to sanitationmen. The cost of this giveaway came to better than $150 million, and no one could be sure that marked the end of the line on the prospective payout. The city had a variety of unpersuasive explanations for why it had sewn itself into a straitjacket from which there was no possibility of escape without frightful cost. It had been plain from the beginning that not even an Albert Einstein could balance out an equation that called for patrolmen and firemen to get equivalent pay and did the same for police sergeants and fire lieutenants when one department had a contractual ratio of 3 to 3.5 and the other of 3 to 3.9. The obvious answer was that the mayor, with a tough election battle coming up, had instructed his bargaining team to avoid a strike at any price—and that had been the price.

What made it all even worse, in a period when the city was begging in Albany for extra state aid and taxing authority to plug a billion-dollar hole in its 1971-72 budget, was that the pot of gold the uniformed services got out of the parity grab-bag did not count at all in the unions' computations of what they ought to get in new money in the 1971 contract.

PENSION TROUBLES

But a factor even more troublesome than the need for fiscal austerity got in the way of wrapping up the police-fire-sanitation negotiations—an acute attack of "me-tooism" in the pension field. Here again politics reared its ugly head, but that was nothing new in determining how much old-age security New York should provide for its unionized employees.

New York State law provides that the legislature must approve any changes in municipal pension plans that make them more generous than the retirement system the state has established for its own employees. The State Constitution seals in improvements; once made, they can never be revoked. The involvement these provisions give Albany in the pension process taught the New York City unions long ago that there were advantages to be gained from making occasional end runs to the state capital and thus getting pension adjustments they could not wring from City Hall.

This doubledecking gambit had been used by the police and fire unions in 1968 to get from Governor Rockefeller, over Mayor Lindsay's objections, a cost-of-living escalator to jack up pensions for their retired members. Five years earlier these same unions had gone behind Mayor Wagner's back to win legislative authorization for a bill basing pension payments on a worker's final salary, including all overtime and other premiums. The State Chamber of Commerce filed a lawsuit to invalidate the law as a breach of home rule. The unions ran to the mayor and, even though he had initially opposed the change, he agreed to amend the city's administrative code so that the gains would stand whether or not the state law survived the court challenge. That ended the lawsuit.

A somewhat similar maneuver sparked the escalation in municipal pensions that caused a major upheaval in the city's labor relations in mid-1971. DeLury had started it in 1965 by getting a commitment from Wagner, shortly before he left office, to go along with a pension system for sanitation employees that would give them the right to retire at half-pay after twenty years' service, regardless of age. Policemen and firemen had previously been the only ones with that privilege, a recognition of the hazardous nature of their duties.

The liberalized retirement plan for sanitationmen slipped through the legislature the following year, almost unnoticed. Lindsay took the view that he had to honor his predecessor's pledge and interposed no objection. Not surprisingly, the DeLury breakthrough brought demands from every other civil service union for comparable protection. The Transport Workers Union got a twenty-year, half-pay system in 1968, but the minimum retirement age was fixed at 50. The step-up in benefits prompted 7,000 of the transit system's most skilled employees to retire in the next two years—an exodus that messed up maintenance and made subway riding more dangerous than ever before.

As the pattern of higher pension payments spread, the city also agreed to a substantial cut in employee contributions until they dropped close to the vanishing point. Workers also got full federal Social Security and in some cases city-paid annuities on top of their pensions. What tore it was an agreement negotiated by District Council 37 in 1970 for its citywide unit of 120,000 clerks, administrators, and a comparative handful of blue-collar employees. The talks went on without fanfare or muscle-flexing. The outcome: a plan that entitled workers to a 2.5 percent pay credit for every year of service—half-pay after twenty years, three-quarter pay after thirty years, and full pay after forty. White-collar workers could retire at age 55, blue-collar workers at 50. The plan included full Social Security, but no triple-deck annuity.

The police and fire unions, smoldering ever since DeLury had achieved pension parity with them five years earlier, made no secret of their belief that the granting to District Council 37 of a plan that was in many ways superior to anyone else's represented a political payoff to Gotbaum, the chief mobilizer of labor backing and funds for Lindsay in the 1969 campaign.

Politics or not, the police and fire groups vowed their determination to move back out in front of "the pencil pushers" and reassert their old supremacy over all other municipal unions. They asked for half-pay pensions after fifteen years and full pay after thirty or thirty-five years. Before that issue came to a showdown, Albany got into the act. The governor and the leaders of the Republican-controlled legislature became concerned that state employees would insist on benefits as substantial as those the city had agreed to give the Gotbaum union if the state gave its required assent to the city's deal. A sister union of Council 37, representing 8,000 of the state's 125,000 workers, already had put in for a carbon copy of the New York City plan. A fact-finding panel under the Taylor Act held that the plan far exceeded anything in government or private employment, and recommended against it. Actually, the legislature three years before had put its own members and their staffs under a retirement program roughly the same as that Council 37 had gotten. It even included in the salary base for pensions the "lulus" the legislators got in lieu of expenses. But the lawmakers contended that the cozy arrangement they had worked out for themselves ought not be considered a general precedent for state employees. Their jobs, they said, had to be recognized as "hazardous" in the same sense as those of state troopers. After all, weren't state senators and assemblymen subject to sudden death at the hands of the voters?

In any event, neither the governor nor the GOP legislative chiefs had any love for Gotbaum. He had been as active in opposing Rockefeller in 1970 as he had in backing Lindsay in 1969. Out of this mélange of politics and of fear that both city and state would eventually be bankrupted by pension escalation (even before the liberalization of the plans for Council 37 and the United Federation of Teachers, the city alone was spending $625 million a year on pensions), the Albany leaders decided to put the Gotbaum program in cold storage while they awaited a report from a special commission set up to study all public pension plans in the state.

The Council 37 head, not normally one to wave his fists, decided to call "the biggest, fattest, sloppiest strike" in the city's history to force the legislature's hand. In alliance with a Teamsters Union local representing bridgetenders, the council initiated a two-day exhibition of urban guerrilla warfare that sent 700 million gallons of raw sewage spewing into metropolitan waterways, shut down garbage incinerators, cut off school lunches for needy children, and made a shambles of traffic by locking two dozen city bridges in uncrossable positions.

The union asserted that its only goal was to induce the legislature to say yes or no to its plan, but the torrent of public condemnation directed at the strike by angry New Yorkers made it easy for the governor and the GOP high command in Albany to stand firm in their resolve to shelve the whole issue until 1972. The mayor publicly renewed earlier pleas for a legislative green light, but most observers were convinced that his private reaction was one of considerable delight that Albany had taken the city off another spot that might have proved as uncomfortable as the one it had got itself into by its improvident deal on police parity pay.

The OCB provided the facesaver Gotbaum needed to extricate himself from a strike he had threatened to keep escalating until the legislature acted. Under its settlement formula, the city promised to resubmit the pension plan for approval next year. If the legislature refused to clear it, the city and the union would try to negotiate a substitute acceptable to Albany. Failing that, the city and the union would work out a plan that did not require legislative review—within the cost limits originally calculated for the higher pensions.

Legislative Backlash

The Gotbaum contretemps was not the only indication at the 1971 legislative session that the lawmakers felt the time had come to put a lid on skyrocketing civil service labor costs and on the extension of union power into the determination of basic public policy. The legislature rushed through, heedless of union protests, a law intended to put a stopper on the wide open door it and the city had combined to unlock for inflating pensions through heavy overtime and other premiums in an employee's last year. A 20 percent ceiling was put on such extra payments in future pension agreements. The lawmakers also decreed that municipalities would have to tell how much money would be needed to pay for the pensions they negotiated and where the money was going to come from. As a further step toward fiscal responsibility, cities were ordered to put all funding for pensions on a current basis, instead of deferring the initial contributions for two or three years.

Of even greater long-range significance was a bill that popped up in the session's closing days to build a fence around the bargaining table —one that would shut out issues the legislators felt ought to be the sole prerogative of elected officials. Among the taboo items would be bargaining on government programs or school curricula, the qualifications of employees, the number of workers to be hired, the fixing of teacher-pupil ratios in schools, rules governing promotion, discipline and assignment, job standards, and the classification of jobs, existing or new. The inclusiveness of this list evoked such a concentrated barrage of labor opposition that the GOP leaders decided not to press the measure this year. A more refined substitute almost certainly will come up in 1972 with strong leadership backing.

Indications for Future

DIMINISHING MANAGEMENT RIGHTS

It is in this area of the scope of bargaining that bitter battles lie ahead for New York City's ultra-political labor movement. Every union contract is a limit on management's freedom, and nowhere is that tug-of-war more difficult to resolve than in governmental service. Everything a teachers' union does affects the quality of education, and in New York the cross-over from straight bread-and-butter concerns to the nature of the educational system is profound. The United Federation of Teachers was not only dominant in the legislative hassle over school decentralization but it incorporated into its contracts a provision for double-manned "More Effective Schools" as the chief vehicle for educational reform. The extent to which such incursions into policy determination would be prohibited by the proposed curbs in Albany has already prompted the UFT to fuse its strength with that of other teacher groups all over the state to mount a militant counteroffensive next year.

Realistically, no legal walls are going to keep civil service unions from moving increasingly into the policy field. Private industry learned many years ago that unions are ingenious enough to find a hundred expedients for punching holes in "management's rights" clauses. Manpower is so much a bedrock of all municipal services that public unions will find ways to tie considerations of job security or working conditions into every policy issue they want to have a voice in.

Racial and Ethnic Pressures

Equally vexing in the years ahead will be efforts to resolve another central question: Can municipal agencies—strapped in the twin rigidities of unionization and the civil service—adapt swiftly enough to the explosive pressures of Negroes and Puerto Ricans for more city jobs and for more direct involvement in every phase of neighborhood service, from schools and hospitals to police and fire protection?

Lindsay's whole effort since he got to City Hall has been to take the abrasive edges off this inescapable conflict by trying to persuade the militants on the Negro side that an orderly transfer of power can be effected without confrontations that trample on the rights of whites to build up rights for blacks. The mayor's approach entails giving the people who are interested in change a voice in change.

To many white workers, especially those whose municipal jobs expose them to daily danger and insult on the police beat or the fire engine or in the tumultuous school system, this mayoral attitude seems a go-ahead for black supremacists and vigilantes. The civil service union leader, worried enough in his own right, finds a new dimension added to his merchandising problem as salesmen for any agreement he negotiates with the city. "Dump Lindsay" was the sign the teachers carried at City Hall. "Dump Lindsay" was the slogan for the policemen, too.

"GIMME"

Political vindictiveness, fear, and race hate thus inflame the difficulties already created by the "gimme" spirit that is rampant in every union, public or private. The man with a good civil service job feels as pushed around as the man without one. The policeman spurns a $14,150-a-year pay offer because he feels he ought to be supreme in the municipal wage system. The hospital or housing worker in the $6,000 category insists he would be better off on relief. The mother on relief demands department-store credit cards to supplement the public payments that give a welfare family of four an annual cash income of $4,000 and that will cost taxpayers in the neighborhood of $2 billion in this fiscal year. The taxpayers, including a growing number who work for the city, get away from it all, at least part of the time, by moving across the city line to Westchester, New Jersey or Long Island. And the city's streets are full of Rolls-Royces, Cadillacs, and Jaguars. Gleaming new office buildings mushroom in midtown. Cooperatives on the fashionable East Side sell for upward of $100,000. Tiffany's and Cartier's are as crowded as supermarkets.

HYPOCRITICAL DISREGARD FOR THE LAW

Those who stand on either side of the municipal barricades wrap themselves in a mantle of self-righteousness and justify their excesses by pointing to the abuses of everyone else. Laws are something for other people to obey, an attitude that applies to alarmed white unionists and embattled black extremists alike. The ultimate idiocy was the way in which both sides in the Ocean Hill controversy hung out the banner of "due process" as a cover for their actions, while each used illegal tactics to make its position stick.

Injunctions issued under the no-strike provisions of the state's Taylor Law are treated like scrap paper by all the major municipal unions except police and fire, and even these sworn upholders of law and order have stopped deferring to the law. Yet none of this seems relevant to any union chief as a possible explanation for the heedlessness of law exhibited by ghetto militants when they clash with the police on school steps or in the streets.

MANAGEMENT ALERTNESS

The essential lesson of New York City's whole experience is that there is no substitute for alertness on the part of the elected officials once they embark on the basically sound proposition that the city's best interests will be served by giving civil service unions negotiating rights comparable to those which prevail in industry. If managerial slackness, ineptitude or politics blunt the relationship, the community will become captive of its unionized employees.

Even now Isaiah Robinson, Jr., newly elected black president of the citywide Board of Education, charges that the unions dwarf the board in political muscle. He predicts that the merger of the UFT with the State Teachers Association and other independent groups will enable the amalgamated organization to "dictate" educational policy not only in the city but all over the state.

Albert Shanker, UFT president, once a firm believer in Bayard Rustin's doctrine that a coalition of labor and civil rights organizations represents the best insurance of progressive governmental policies, acknowledges that trends toward black separatism have banished that faith. The acid fruits of just such mutual antagonisms almost destroyed Newark, just across the Hudson, in a 1971 school strike so bitter it made Ocean Hill-Brownsville seem a play-school project. Newark's Negro Mayor, Kenneth Gibson, was chiefly responsible for keeping the local teachers' union from being smashed in that strike, but the hatred for the union that surfaced among dominant elements in the black community made its long-term survival a poor bet.

EMPLOYEE EXODUS FROM CITY

An ironic factor undermining the concentrated political punch of New York's civil service unions is the heightening degree to which their members are joining the exodus to the suburbs. If all 380,000 municipal employees actually lived inside the city, they and their families would roughly match the 1.2 million persons on welfare. That would mean 30 percent of the city's population living on tax revenue, without counting pensioners dependent on Social Security and other government retirement systems. However, it is probable that a third of the municipal employees now live outside the five boroughs. The ratio is higher for policemen, firemen, and teachers. The better the job, the less likely the employee is to live in the city—and the greater the resentment of the impoverished ghetto resident who cannot understand why the job should not be his.

The votes of these absent unionists cannot be mobilized to elect a mayor their union likes or to defeat one it detests. Nevertheless, the line-up of the municipal unions in 1969 did reflect a considerable allegiance to the fast-swelling payroll. Lindsay, running for reelection without either the Democratic or the Republican designation, had such old Wagner stalwarts as the sanitation union and the TWU lined up with District Council 37 in his campaign train, even though Van Arsdale and the Central Labor Council strung along with the Democrats. It might have been different had Van Arsdale succeeded in his vigorous attempt to get Wagner into the mayoralty contest, but the former mayor fell by the wayside in the primary.

THREAT OF STRIKES

Another element in the politicalization of New York's civil service bargaining is the extent to which the delicate fabric of community can be mangled by a strike involving a comparative handful of unionized workers. The 1971 strike over state approval of pensions, which made life miserable for millions of city residents and commuters alike, involved only 8,000 strategically placed blue-collar employees out of a total unit of 120,000.

Gotbaum had been at pains beforehand to stress that the strike's sole aim was to harass wealthy suburbanites, the bedrock of the political constituency represented by Governor Rockefeller and the GOP legislative leaders. But no such tidy rationing of political punishment resulted. The bridge tieup caused more hardship for truck drivers and ribbon clerks than for the owners of chauffeur-driven limousines. And everything after that as the noose was tightened—the incipient pollution of metropolitan beaches with untreated sewage, the withholding of school lunches—pinched the windpipe of the poor.

The clear need in New York—as in all cities with advanced bargaining systems—is for the development of collective relationships that will take the bulldozing out of labor relations. Whatever appropriateness such methods still have in private industry, they have none where all the people are the employer and the viability of the community is so much in doubt. Public employees will not be supplicants at the community table, but they cannot be dictators either.

William B. Gould

10

Labor Relations and Race Relations

Public Unions' Opportunity

Collective bargaining is relatively new to public employment and so are the public unions. Perhaps the foremost problem of these new unions in race relations will be to avoid the racially discriminatory practices which have been committed by private sector unions over these many years. It is my opinion that these emerging public unions have a fresh opportunity in the race relations field which they should not let slip away.

This assumption is buttressed by the fact that the American Federation of State, County and Municipal Employees (AFSCME) represents a substantial number of the disproportionately high percentage of black employees in public employment. As Professor Ewart Guinier, chairman of the Harvard University Afro-American Studies Department, has said: ". . . in 1935 (during the CIO drive) . . . a new union of municipal workers, the State, County and Municipal Workers [AFSCME], evinced an interest in black workers, appointed blacks as organizers, elected blacks to leadership positions, and took up the special grievances of blacks with municipal administrations throughout the country."

Today AFSCME is not the only employee union with a relatively progressive record in the race area. In part, this phenomenon is

WILLIAM B. GOULD *is visiting professor of law at Harvard Law School and has been professor of law at Wayne State University Law School since 1968. He has been in the private practice of labor law and has served on the legal staffs of the United Automobile Workers and the National Labor Relations Board. Professor Gould has also acted as legal consultant to both the United States Equal Employment Opportunity Commission and the National Association for the Advancement of Colored People.*

attributable to the fact that blacks appear to be more significant, both politically and statistically, in the public sector than in private employment. Traditionally, government has been a job market where minorities could obtain access more easily than in private industry. Accordingly, as Bayard Rustin has noted, a large number of black government workers "such as hospital workers, sanitation workers, farm workers, and paraprofessionals in educational and social welfare institutions" have recently joined public unions.

UNION RESPONSIBILITY TO FIGHT DISCRIMINATION

But there remain very serious obstacles to racial equality in public employment—especially higher level positions, where the number of blacks is small—and there are departments of local government, such as police and fire, with few blacks employed on any basis and an even smaller number in high paying positions of responsibility. The labor movement cannot avoid some responsibility for this pattern. Victor Gotbaum, the AFSCME District 37 director, has said: "Let's not kid ourselves. . . . They don't like us in the black community. We have to make a determined analysis why this is so and do something about it. Labor may be doing as much as other groups, but that isn't enough. We're supposed to be the friend of the underdog."

What is the responsibility of public employee unions in racial discrimination in government? There is a broad range of response. Some unions bristle at the notion that they have any. Their attitude is that they represent the employees and have no responsibility for the hiring policies of the public employer with which they bargain. They reflect the composition of the work force rather than seek to revise it. Yet the duty of fair representation cases in the private sector seems to say that a labor organization has an obligation to act affirmatively on behalf of employees who are not presently employed within the bargaining unit (see United States Supreme Court, *Brotherhood of Railway Trainmen v. Howard,* 1952, and *Phelps Dodge Corp. v. NLRB,* 1941; and NLRB, *Tanner Motor Livery, Ltd.,* 1967). It is quite possible that the courts will impose an obligation upon unions in both the public and private sector to negotiate and police affirmative action hiring policies. Unions recognize that national labor policy and the courts already require that they represent members fairly and not discriminate in the representation as between black and white members. This is significant in pursuing grievances over working conditions, promotions, and the like. Some of the public unions, such as AFSCME, recognize that both as a matter of principle and of winning the loyal support of union members from minority groups, it is necessary to press for affirmative action to hire more minority employees and to encourage promotions from this part of the work force.

Whatever the attitude of the union, change in the municipal, state or federal work force is not easy, for one of the great attractions of public service traditionally has been job security, job tenure, and seniority as a major consideration in promotion. Present government employees, and their union spokesmen, are not inclined to narrow these employment protections.

PUBLIC EMPLOYERS' ATTITUDES

Public employers, too, vary in their attitudes. Some chief executives of larger, older cities recognize that recent population shifts have changed the racial composition of their communities and that some affirmative action is necessary to revise the makeup of the city work force. They have adopted some of the procedures of the industrial world in recruiting, qualifying, training, and promoting minority representatives. While none speak of a quota system, they are becoming increasingly aware of the disparity between the percentage of blacks in the big cities and their representation in municipal employment. Some effort has been made in staffing police departments—an activity where blacks on the force bring an extra qualification to law enforcement and an activity where expansion permits additions without tossing incumbents out.

But even with this effort, it is clear that there is yet much to be done. An August 1971 tabulation showed:

	Black Population	Police		Black Population	Police
Atlanta	51.3%	10%	Minneapolis	4%	1%
Chicago	33%	16.2%	Newark	80%	14%
Cleveland	40%	7%	New York	31%	8.5%
Dallas	25%	2%	Oakland	40%	6.5%
Detroit	45%	13%	Phoenix	5%	2%
Los Angeles	17.9%	5%	St. Louis	41%	14.8%
Miami	22.7%	11%	Washington	70%	37%

In one major city the public employer has found both allies and enemies in various unions as he set out to put more blacks in publicly visible posts. The problem of changing the work force is not simple. Progressive public employers accept the principle of collective bargaining; they deal with the chosen representatives of their employees. If the vast majority of these are white, their representatives are likely to be, too, and unlikely to welcome any policies or actions detrimental to their constituency. How to break this cycle is a real challenge.

Discrimination in Promotions

In the industrial world, racial discrimination has a long and sordid history. This is less clear in government *hiring*—as distinguished from promotion—because blacks have been employed in government in large numbers due to both political pressure and the fact that whites have often preferred jobs in private industry, from which blacks were traditionally excluded. The most virulent forms of discrimination in the public sector arise in the promotion context. This has often been effectuated through the wide use of written examinations as a basis for determining who is to be promoted as well as hired.

In Detroit and San Francisco, for instance, entry into any job outside the laborer classification in municipal government necessitates a written examination. While such tests may or may not actually determine who can perform the job, they appear to screen out blacks disproportionately to whites. Moreover, if, as often proves to be the case, the public employer selects the first person on the list of applicants who have taken a test—or the individual with the highest test score—this may have an adverse impact upon blacks or other minorities who are able to meet the basic standards relevant to adequate performance, but are not skilled in taking tests. Often passing scores, which are not the very best, are nullified through the scrapping of waiting lists consisting of those who passed the tests, but had not been placed on jobs.

LEGAL DEVELOPMENTS

The evolving law against racial discrimination in employment means that a substantial attack upon testing in public employment is just beginning. And even those unions like AFSCME are uncertain about how to respond to the challenge, whether to support the status quo or attack it.

The leading case in this area is *Griggs v. Duke Power Company,* where a unanimous Supreme Court held that a standardized general intelligence test used as a condition of employment and for job transfer violates Title VII of the Civil Rights Act of 1964 when blacks have been discriminated against in the past, and the test is not "significantly" related to successful job performance. Said Chief Justice Burger, speaking for the Court: "If an employment practice which operates to exclude Negroes cannot be shown to be related to job performance, the practice is prohibited. . . . Good intent or absence of discriminatory intent does not redeem employment procedures or testing mechanisms that operate 'built-in headwinds' for minority groups and are unrelated to measuring job capability."

Title VII, as it is presently written, does not apply to public employment. But the lower courts have already begun to apply much of the same kind of analysis to the public employer's obligations under the Equal Protection Clause of the Fourteenth Amendment. In New York City a recent federal court ruling invalidating examinations for school principals, and the defense of such procedures provided by both the Council of Supervisors and Administrators and the United Federation of Teachers (UFT), make it clear that some public employee unions, like the crafts, support culturally devised and nonjob-related tests in the name of preserving "standards."

COMMUNITY INTERESTS AND UNION LEADERSHIP

Also of paramount importance in any consideration of the relationship between public employee unions and minority groups is the relationship between the service performed and the community. The black community often has a dual complaint against the unions. On the one hand unions have been a party to exclusion of minorities for police, fire, and teaching jobs; and on the other hand, white union members have been heavy-handed and insensitive in delivering municipal services to low-income blacks. That the unions can be caught up in this kind of conflict was visibly demonstrated by the 1968 Ocean Hill-Brownsville strike in New York City and the unpopularity accorded the United Federation of Teachers because of its role in that dispute. While arbitrary transfer procedures established by the local governing board triggered this dispute, it had its genesis in smoldering black resentment against what was viewed as insensitivity by white teachers who were union members. This led to the view that black principals and black teachers, for the most part, were necessary to provide effective service.

Finally, the fact that some unions in the public sector with an increasingly large black membership retain lily-white leadership at the national levels is irritating. An example of this situation is the Amalgamated Transit Union (ATU) which includes drivers and mechanics for public transit. Some of the tensions between that organization's leadership and the rank and file are undoubtedly attributable to the absence of black representation for the union's black members. Both AFSCME and the American Federation of Teachers (AFT) have done considerably better in integrating their leadership positions.

Indeed, the performance of these two unions may be superior to any labor organization that represents employees in the private sector as well as the public. In seeming contrast, one finds the American Federation of Government Employees (AFGE), the dominant labor organization in federal government, which represents both blue and white collar workers and has a membership in excess of 20 percent minority. The union has only one black executive board member.

BLACK CAUCUSES

It is situations such as this and a growing feeling by black union members that their interests and concerns are not being adequately dealt with that have brought about a growing number of racially separate groups or racial caucuses within national and local unions or employee associations. In Detroit, for example, black police officers organized The Guardians, which proposed to the leadership of the Detroit Police Officers Association that key posts be apportioned so that all races were represented. The reasoning behind this proposal is that blacks are not able to get elected to association office by votes of the predominantly white membership in the Detroit Police Department and that only positive support for blacks by white leaders will alter this. They argue that the absence of blacks from leadership positions reflects the same bias which is presumed where minorities have token or no representation in the work force. Accordingly, they continue, as the courts have imposed affirmative action obligations upon unions and employers, the public unions, if they are serious about dealing with racial discord, ought to affirmatively recruit black leadership.

Finally, the racial problem in public employment cannot be completely understood without reference to the United States Postal Service and the existence of the National Alliance of Postal Employees, a predominantly black organization formed in 1913 to protect black employees against racial discrimination in that department as well as exclusion then from membership by white postal unions. The Alliance purportedly has a membership of 45,000—but most of the members also have cards now in other unions. Existing unit determinations have squeezed the Alliance out of the coalition of unions bargaining with the Postal Service under the Postal Reorganization Act. Under that statute, the National Labor Relations Board (NLRB) will have to decide whether the Alliance can gain bargaining rights for some of its members. This issue foreshadows future tensions between predominantly white labor organizations and black employee organizations which speak for minority employees concerning some aspects of the employment relationship.

Experience in Several Employment Sectors

One day when men and women of all races have achieved equal access to jobs and equal opportunity for promotion and policy-making and can work for government in harmony, the need for union structures separated by the color line will no longer be clear. Until that time, we must recognize that workers will feel they have to join together within unions to advance their group cause. To understand the strong feelings of black city workers, a look at several unions with substantial black membership is useful.

TRANSIT WORKERS

Most of the big city transit systems are in the public sector. In 1970, Equal Employment Opportunity Commission statistics collected for Atlanta, Chicago, Detroit, Los Angeles, Philadelphia, and Washington, D.C., indicated that 33.6 percent of all employees and 37.6 percent of the blue collar workers in the urban transit industry were black.

Because whites do not seek transit employment in large numbers— urban crime being a factor in this—blacks have gained substantial employment even without affirmative action recruiting policies. In Detroit a majority of the transit work force is black. Similarly, in New York City a majority of the workers are black or Puerto Rican, with approximately 40 percent of the employees being black. It is estimated that of approximately 1,500 new employees hired by the New York City Transit Authority during the past two years, between 1,100 and 1,200 were black. In Houston and Washington the percentage of Negro employees is in excess of 40 percent. In Chicago and Los Angeles, it is in excess of 30 percent and in Philadelphia the percentage is approximately 25 percent.

As of 1970 approximately 22 percent of the transit industry's craftsmen were Negroes—a figure that compares most favorably with other industries. As is the case with minority employees in transit generally, the figures have moved upward quite recently. Black craftsmen were "scarce" in the transit industry as of 1966. One of the reasons was the absence of company apprenticeship programs and the recruitment of the craftsmen from other industries rather than upgrading of lower level transit employees. But then the shortage of craftsmen forced the transit companies to train and upgrade Negroes.

Despite the substantial black participation in big city transit operations, the General Executive Board of the Amalgamated Transit Union, AFL-CIO, is lily-white. While there are discussions being undertaken relating to the feasibility of electing a black board member and while union officials express some concern about the racial composition of leadership, there are no clear signs that the status quo will be altered in this regard.

At the same time, there are a small number of local union officials who are black: Cleveland (president); Detroit (secretary-treasurer); Washington (president of Local 1528, the Airport Transport Local); Baltimore (secretary-treasurer); Chicago (Local 308, Rapid Transit, president, and Local 241, buses, secretary-treasurer).

Black caucuses are forming in Amalgamated locals such as Washington, Richmond, and Norfolk. According to ATU officials, representatives of the Washington black caucus refused to run for office even though the leadership desired a more racially balanced executive board.

In Chicago, until 1968 there were only four Negro members on a 28-man executive board and no black amongst the full-time leadership. Blacks comprise the majority of the membership, but the union permits retirees to vote in elections and almost all such retirees are white.

The Concerned Transit Workers (CTW), an organization of black workers formed primarily to achieve more black leadership in Division 241 of ATU in Chicago, engaged in two wildcat stoppages in July and August of that year. The CTW's preoccupation with the issue of leadership was triggered by the announcement of Division President James Hill that he was resigning his position as president to become financial secretary of the international union. The stoppages appeared to be aimed primarily at the elimination of the white retirees' vote which was, according to the CTW's officials, excluding blacks from union office. Subsequent to the second walkout, approximately 100 black workers were discharged by the Chicago Transit Authority (CTA), and this seems to have demolished the CTW's organizational effort.

However, in the wake of the wildcat stoppages in 1968, one full-time black official, James Pate, was elected financial secretary-treasurer of Division 241. It is arguable that the tensions caused by the CTW's efforts in Chicago contributed to this. On the other hand, it should also be noted that the president of Chicago Division 308, which has jurisdiction over the rapid transit workers, is black and was recently elected without any turmoil. Four of the seven members of Division 308's executive board are now black. But prior to the 1969 elections, the only black union leader was an assistant board member.

Detroit is substantially different from Chicago—probably because of its larger black membership and also because the public employer was hiring blacks into bus driver jobs as early as 1941 and 1942. For the past decade there has been a majority of black drivers and black union leadership in Division 26, which represents black transit workers in Detroit.

The first black officer in a full-time position in Detroit—and, for that matter, in any ATU local—was Lee Halley, financial secretary-treasurer, who was elected in 1958 when the black membership was approximately a third of the total. He has won reelection ever since that time. Today, four out of five major offices are held by blacks and only the president is white.

According to Halley, the union has pressed hard for promotion of blacks into supervisory positions outside the bargaining unit. While there appears to be less tension inside the union than in Chicago, Detroit blacks have linked with full-time Negro officers in ATU locals in Chicago, Cleveland, and Washington to put pressure upon the national union to support a black candidate for executive board member.

The Transport Workers Unions of America (TWU), ATU's principal rival, was affiliated with the CIO before the latter's merger with the AF of L. This union has established civil rights machinery, but some charge that segregation and discrimination have existed in TWU locals. Nonetheless, there appears to be more black representation in TWU than ATU. On the international level, there are two elected black vice-presidents, Charles Faulding and Roosevelt Watts. The executive board of the international has eight blacks out of 27 elected members. However, there is black caucus activity in the locals of San Francisco and New York City.

I am of the view that black participation in union decision making is an integral part of the establishment of fair employment patterns. Even in the absence of appreciable changes in hiring and promotions, the presence of blacks among union leaders helps assure fairness to minorities.

TEACHERS

The American Federation of Teachers expelled those locals which insisted upon segregation shortly after the Supreme Court's decision in *Brown v. Board of Education*. The leadership continues to speak out in support of recent desegregation decisions of the Court. The AFT has one of the most racially balanced leaderships in the labor movement. Approximately four of the 22-member Executive Board of the American Federation of Teachers are black although the black membership is substantially smaller than the ATU, which has not elected any Negroes at the national level. Locally AFT has not fared well in New York City, Newark, and Chicago black-white disputes, and there is dissatisfaction with the national leadership of AFT as well as of some locals on the part of black AFT members.

In the New York City strike involving the dispute at Ocean Hill Brownsville, which pitted the New York City UFT leadership against that district's advocates of community control, black community leaders as well as some Negro members of the UFT attacked the Federation's position as unresponsive to the black community. In part, this conflict now centers upon the AFT's support of tests for teacher applicants which others agree are not job related. It is to be noted that this position seems contrary to the one taken by the Federation's rival, the National Education Association (NEA).

In Chicago, the Federation's seniority provisions in its collective bargaining agreement with the Chicago Board of Education are linked to efforts to desegregate the public school system. In both Chicago and New York the effect of seniority provisions negotiated by the Federation is to permit experienced and well paid teachers to transfer to districts which they regard as less troublesome and which, more often than not, are not those in which blacks reside. This seniority is also related to the implementation of Federal Judge Skelly Wright's decision ordering equalization of school expenditures between rich and poor, white and black neighborhoods in Washington, D.C.

New York City, Chicago, and Washington, D.C., appear to have much of the same problem. But in Detroit the seniority system is not so rigid. Assignments are made on the basis of a number of factors

such as seniority, racial composition of the faculty and school, and the
experience that a particular teacher has accumulated.

POLICE

The percentage of black policemen in large urban areas with a substantial Negro population has been a subject of much discussion.
While gains have been made, more may be indicated where cities are
beset by tensions between the police and black populations and where
a disproportionate percentage of crime occurs in the inner city or
ghetto. Washington, with the largest percentage of blacks in any major
city, has made the most progress in recruiting black police.

As Paul Delaney of *The New York Times* stated in 1971:

> Four years ago, blacks made up only 17 percent of the Capital's 4,300
> men. In September, 1968, the percentage was up to 24.4 percent, or 786
> blacks of 3,207 men. By last August 1,000 more blacks have been added for
> a total of 1,797 of 4,994 or 35.9.
>
> Washington did it by setting up recruitmobiles in black sections where
> written examinations were given; recruiting on military basis; changing
> physical standards, such as lowering the height requirement and modifying
> the eye requirement and changing the requirements of certain illnesses
> such as asthma and hay fever; conducting a "recruit-in-moviethon" where
> applicants and their dates attended free showings of Jim Brown and John
> Wayne movies, and a "radiothon" in which applicants were solicited over
> the radio and taxicabs were sent to pick them up and bring them to the
> station to take their test.

The tensions between black police and their white colleagues—particularly the unions or associations which represent them—are many.
One source of conflict is to be found in the use of the written examination and the view of black police that such procedures are an obstacle
to the recruitment of new black policemen. For instance, in Detroit in
1967, 50 percent of the Negroes and 17 percent of the whites taking
the written examination failed it.

A number of black police organizations have been formed. There
are so-called Guardian organizations in Detroit, New York, and Philadelphia. In Chicago, an extremely militant group calls itself the Afro-
American Patrolmen's League (AAPL) and in Washington there is a
National Black Caucus. There are very few black policemen in leadership positions in the police officers associations in these cities. However, in Newark and Philadelphia there are black second vice-
presidents in the fraternal police organizations. And in Washington
the president of the Police Association of Washington is black.

As of this time, there appears to be no effort by any of these black
police organizations to represent blacks in the grievance machinery.
Nor does there appear to be any attempt to supplant the machinery
with separate procedures for blacks. But in Newark, since the election

of Mayor Kenneth A. Gibson a year ago, black police have tended to bypass the Patrolmen's Benevolent Association (PBA) inasmuch as the mayor has an "open door" policy. The Chicago AAPL maintains a two-man legal staff which challenges suspensions and represents members at hearings.

FIRE FIGHTERS

According to the United States Commission on Civil Rights, discrimination in fire departments in many cities is ". . . similar to, and in many ways worse, than those in police departments." Here also, promotion for minority group members and written and oral examinations pose a major barrier. The Commission said in 1969:

> There are three ways in which the situation in the fire department study were significantly different from those of the police departments. First, most fire departments are not understaffed, have a small turnover, and have no trouble getting applicants. Second, the relationship between the fire department and the minority community is not as tense and hostile as in the case of the police. Third, the unusual working arrangement of firemen has given rise to many forms of prejudiced attitudes and treatment.

The tensions between the black community and fire fighters have increased since the commission's report. It is estimated that throughout the United States approximately 97 to 98 percent of all fire fighters are whites. And some of the most antisocial elements in the ghetto have heaped substantial physical and verbal abuse upon the fire fighters who are called into the Negro community quite often.

Although the percentage of black fire fighters is smaller than black police, here also blacks have begun to form their own organization outside of the International Association of Fire Fighters, AFL-CIO. Among the most prominent is the Detroit Phoenix Organization, formed after the 1967 riots. Phoenix, unlike the Detroit Guardians police group, has apparently excluded whites from membership. On issues which it regards as having racial implications, Phoenix encourages its black fire fighter members to go directly to the chief executive of the department, City Hall, or the Common Council. As with police, the focus of attack seems to be what are regarded as discriminatory hiring qualifications, such as the requiring of a high school diploma and passing a written examination. However, the personal interview requirement has now been dropped and Phoenix has been intrumental in getting the maximum height requirement as well as the driver's license requirement eliminated.

FEDERAL EMPLOYEES

Most blacks and other minorities hold the lower level positions in the federal government, as in state and local counterparts. The United

States Civil Service Commission has ultimate authority over equal employment opportunity matters but it rarely reverses the decisions of department heads concerning disputes in this area. Accordingly, recent legislative proposals have, as one of their objectives, the granting of jurisdiction over federal equal employment opportunity to the United States Equal Employment Opportunity Commission rather than the Civil Service Commission. This has the sensible objective of making certain that an independent agency which is exclusively committed to the goals of civil rights legislation will have final authority (along with the federal courts) to adjudicate complaints of discrimination.

What is the attitude of the unions in the federal sector? The most important and largest union, representing both blue and white collar workers, the American Federation of Government Employees (AFGE), has recently established a civil rights department which is concerned with affirmative action. But it is clear that the activity of the national union to date involves mostly seminars and discussions with local union people. All of this, of course, is important. But AFGE does not appear to involve itself in any substantive issues concerning discrimination or lack of affirmative action at the union local level. Accordingly, there appears to be some dissatisfaction with AFGE and other federal unions on the part of the blacks.

Quite recently, approximately 100 blacks voted to quit General Accounting Office Local 8 of AFGE, charging racism on the part of the union because the local did not act on 80 membership applications filed by the blacks until after the local union elections. Only one executive board member of AFGE is black. Further, groups of federal employees in the Departments of Housing and Urban Development and Health, Education and Welfare were formed to protest racial discrimination in employment. One result is an organization called Government Employees United Against Racial Discrimination (GUARD) which has engaged in a number of demonstrations. Such activity has perplexed federal officials who are uncertain about the extent to which they may consult and negotiate with such groups in the face of a collective bargaining relationship.

The Postal Service is now outside Executive Order 11491 and its collective bargaining is regulated by the NLRB under the Postal Reorganization Act. One of the prominent issues here is bound to be the status of the National Alliance of Postal Employees which, incidentally, is now attempting to organize other governmental employees and to operate as a pressure group to end discrimination throughout the federal government.

The Alliance's competitors are many. One of the most formidable is the National Post Office Mail Handlers affiliated with the Laborer's Union. Forty-eight percent of its 55,000 membership is black and two of the three national officers are black. One of the other major unions, the United Federation of Postal Clerks, has a membership of approximately 170,000, but only one of its fifteen vice-presidents is black. Shortly, the United Federation of Postal Clerks will merge with several other postal unions.

Conclusion

The public employee unions have a better chance to deal with the problems of racial discrimination because their growth is so recent. Yet, on the federal level, one can predict that large unions like AFGE and the United Postal Clerks may be the objects of considerable criticism on the part of blacks because of their past inactivity and overt discrimination against blacks. Many municipal police and fire organizations may have even more difficulty than the craft unions because they are not only tainted with the brush of a predominantly white work force, but are in continuing conflict with the black community as well.

Yet, because of the comparatively large employment of blacks in many governmental units, the rapid growth of public employees' unions may be an important vehicle for providing blacks a voice in the house of labor. One can see this trend in its beginning stages in connection with the American Federation of State, County and Municipal Employees which is now the seventh largest AFL-CIO union and, indeed, at some point in the future could be the largest. Accordingly, while there is undoubtedly much conflict between the unions and racial minorities around the corner, the public sector may well present the most immediate opportunity for black power in the unions. Indeed where public unions have sought to represent black workers, the black community has rallied to its side. Atlanta, Memphis, Washington, and Detroit helped AFSCME in its collective bargaining struggle.

Sam Zagoria

11

The Future of Collective Bargaining in Government

The longest journey can only begin with the first step. So it is with a chapter—one writes down the title of the chapter and then hopes for inspiration—and good luck. With the above title, one peers into the crystal ball cautiously, recalling the warning of an old friend who counseled, "If at all possible limit predictions to things which should occur beyond your own lifetime."

But now a caution to the reader, too. What is said here is what one believes is likely to happen, rather than what one would like to see happen. Authors, obviously, lack the power to make the two coincide.

Growth

Starting with the safest forecast first—collective bargaining at all levels of government will grow—in numbers, in penetration of geographic areas, and in the range of topics subjected to bargaining.

While there will continue to be large islands of nonrepresentation and numerous subjects *verboten* for discussion, the growth pattern of public unionism of the 1960s will continue unabated in the seventies. This development will have far-reaching consequences for public employers, public workers, and the public generally. The pattern of government employer-employee relations, once like father to son, is more likely to become that of partners, usually pulling together in mutual interest, but periodically falling apart as bitter adversaries. For the old-time public administrator, the change will appear so drastic, it will seem like a revolution in traditional government.

Some public employers act as if nothing has changed. It has. Recent figures gathered by Professor Jack Stieber of Michigan State University indicate that organization among employees in state and local government, even excluding the highly organized public school teachers, is already proportionately higher than in private industry. Stieber, using published data, questionnaires and interviews, finds that more than a third of the state-county-city work force holds membership in unions or employee associations. With teachers added, the percentage is even higher. The comparable figure for the industrial sector is between a fifth and a fourth of the work force represented by unions.

At the federal level, the percentage of employees represented for bargaining reached 58 percent in 1971 and organizing there continues apace.

Significantly, public unions and associations are steadily increasing their percentage of the work force, while union membership in private industry represents a stagnant or actually declining percentage. With current predictions of an estimated 40 percent expansion of local government staffing during the decade of the seventies, the potential for growth remains high for, as several observers have pointed out, public unions do best in large units of government.

The likelihood of expansion of local government is reinforced by the comment of John W. Gardner that:

> Nothing has changed more radically than the old argument between liberals who wanted a strong central government and conservatives who wanted a weak central government. (The conservatives talked states' rights, but they never promoted strong state and local government. They were essentially opposed to all government.) Today the most intelligent liberals and conservatives favor strengthening state and local government, and call for creation of more flexible and effective federal-state-local partnerships. These partnerships cut across all the old arguments. They distribute power and initiative in new ways. They are beginning to be characterized by a new flexibility, a flexibility that frees state and local government to set its own goals and devise its own strategies.

The potential for public union growth is enhanced by the attitudes of elected officials who, by virtue of their office, are often thrust into the role of public employer. Unlike their private employer counterparts—some of whom are still fighting the statutory right of employees to decide whether they want a union to represent them or not—these public employers, accustomed to representing many and varied segments of society, do not as often look on unions as the enemy when employees choose them. Government employers may prefer not to have their employees represented, and indeed may take shrewd steps to make unionization a less attractive alternative, but, generally speaking, once unions arrive on the scene they have not launched all-out attacks to drive them out of town. This means that while union-employer dealings are beset by all the adversary relationships of the private sector they do not involve the repeated illegal conduct of some private employers in firing employees for joining a union. As time goes on and initial labor-management contact grows and matures, government can be further expected to encourage employee exercise of freedom of choice in representation matters.

All of this is not to say that local, state, and federal governmental units have gone out of their way to attract and welcome unions. A look at existing legislation on the subject demonstrates a diverse, piecemeal, and perhaps even begrudging recognition that public workers may desire unionism. A majority of states have enacted enabling legislation to permit cities and counties to recognize and deal with unions; and year by year the list grows for no state, once having granted such powers, has withdrawn them. The federal government is operating under an executive order which grants a modicum of bargaining opportunity to employees but only in the case of the Postal Service does this go the whole route of wages, hours, and conditions of employment.

STATE LEGISLATION

Some observers have seen a relationship between enactment of state law and growth of unionism; and this can be demonstrated. On the other hand, there are many extensive and mature understandings reached in states where the law is blank on the subject. Here informal consultation and discussion, breakfast table understandings, and handshake agreements have taken the place of the formal trappings of the collective bargaining ritual. In some cases, community crises over workers seeking recognition of a union or the exploding of a massive work stoppage has led to legislative activity. But in many states legislation has followed the longer route of careful study by citizen commissions who invariably recognize that unionization is here to stay and that adoption of intelligent ground rules for defining bargaining units, determining the majority will, and providing resources to assist in resolving impasses may well lead to the avoidance of picket-line warfare.

As more states turn to legislation there is bound to be greater recognition of the elected official's dual role as both legislator and employer. The decision in a few states to give municipal employees the right to collective bargaining, but not state employees, or for the federal government to require private employers to recognize and deal with employee-chosen unions on wages and hours, but not to require the same of itself, is unlikely to withstand the test of time. Additionally, the customary authority of state legislative bodies and state and local civil service commissions to set unilaterally various working conditions, pension rights, and the like will also undergo challenge as collective bargaining grows and flexes new strength.

CRAFT OR INDUSTRIAL?

What form of unionism will predominate? This is not easy to guess, but a few signs offer guidance. In the competition between craft and industrial structures, the industrial already has an edge—in membership and in the number of communities and government agencies affected. The American Federation of State, County and Municipal Employees (AFSCME), AFL-CIO, has members engaged in almost all municipal functions except fire fighting and enjoys the largest membership among the public unions in local government. The American Federation of Government Employees (AFGE), AFL-CIO, also cutting across various crafts and skills, is the biggest in representing federal employees. While the craft unions such as International Association of Fire Fighters, AFL-CIO, the two independent police associations, the building trades, the National Education Association (NEA), and the American Federation of Teachers, AFL-CIO, exist and grow, there have nevertheless been rumblings of joint undertakings such as between AFSCME and NEA, which is the largest in the education field. Such joint effort would be another step toward the industrial format. In addition, local and state employee associations, which also tend to follow the industrial route, match or outnumber union memberships in the same field. Even here there have been recent mergers with existing unions in the area. It can be expected that the problem of competing with unions, national in scope and deep in resources, will continue to be a difficult one for the independent association, and only the strongest associations will be able to survive.

The recruiting and merging ability of AFSCME has enabled it to rise from nineteenth to seventh place in membership size within the AFL-CIO in less than a decade. Professor Stieber, author of a Brookings Institution volume on public union growth, suggests AFSCME may "become one of the largest and possibly the largest union in the AFL-CIO." If this comes to pass, the impact of AFSCME's energetic and volatile president, Jerry Wurf, on the overall policies of the nation's labor movement, and particularly its social welfare initiatives, will itself be worthy of a book.

Industrial unionism, of course, has its advantages and disadvantages for both sides of the bargaining table, but on the whole apparently most employers and most employees have found the former outweigh the latter. With one union, rather than several, generally speaking there are fewer negotiations, fewer adjustments to make in wage relationships between bargaining units, and usually more concentration on wages and hours rather than the level of services and other considerations treasured as managerial prerogatives by managements. On the other hand, the area of confrontation is bigger. Of course this would be true, too, if affected unions join hands in a council or coalition for bargaining purposes; a similar situation exists in some cities now where a job action by one unit or union automatically receives full support from other organized employees.

MULTI-EMPLOYER BARGAINING

The possibilities of broadening the bargaining lineup on both sides of the table are attracting increasing attention. In the federal government, the major postal unions have joined their interests in one negotiating agent and the results could influence other possible ventures. The growing activity of state municipal leagues in providing labor relations counsel to cities could logically lead communities in a county or metropolitan area to join efforts at the bargaining table. This is already underway in the Minneapolis-St. Paul metropolitan area. Increasing initiatives by councils of governments to provide areawide services to constituents in various jurisdictions could also lead to moves in this direction.

My own guess is that the first major efforts at multi-employer bargaining are likely to come with school boards for there is so much that is uniform among them—state aid is apportioned to localities under a uniform formula, the qualifications for teaching and administering are fairly standard, present wage standards in an area approximate one another, and the ability to pay of adjoining communities is likely to be fairly close. These factors suggest that both unions and boards stand to gain by reducing the number of individual negotiations and averting the dangers of whip-sawing, me-tooing, and leapfrogging as locals try to outdo or catch up to one another. Both sides can then afford to employ a higher level of expertise for negotiating sessions and free themselves for other useful purposes. In New York State three populous counties have already established a regional bargaining pattern on teacher salary minimums. A similar effort has commenced in Michigan. Initially governmental units may make an effort to develop, in effect, a master contract and remand local issues for negotiation of individual supplemental agreements. If the public sector follows the pattern of private sector multi-employer agreements, some employee benefits may be developed which would not be feasible in single unit relationships—for example, portability of pensions, transferability of vacation or sick leave credits, or even establishment of areawide in-service training programs for specialty employees.

SUPERVISORY UNIONISM

One area in which there is likely to be substantial variation from the private model is involvement of supervisors in unions, almost unheard of in industry and unprotected by the federal legislation covering private sector rank and file employees. In the public sector, however, the lines between supervisor and supervisee are not always clearly drawn, in good part because prior to collective bargaining there was little necessity to do so. Many a supervisor was a supervisor only on payday, and sometimes not even then.

As a result of managerial negligence, many supervisors feel a stronger kinship with their employees than with top management. As governmental units grow in size, many a municipal supervisor has yet to meet his mayor, or many a state employee his governor, or many a federal worker his cabinet member. Some steps are being taken in government to remedy this, i.e., establishment of supervisory clubs, supervisory training, and special treatment of supervisors in such matters as life insurance and leave policy, but there are already many "supervisors"—the title is in challenge—enrolled in unions. This is true in several police and fire departments and recently the AFL-CIO issued a charter for a union of school principals and department heads.

The sharp upturn in strikes against the government has led many managers to give second thoughts to the role and importance of supervisors. As they make contingency plans for partial operation of essential services during stoppages the question of who is likely to show up has led to examination of whether specific employees would line up with, or would pass through, the marching pickets. This, in turn, has led to more realistic efforts to weld supervisors into the management team. To the extent that supervisors are recognized and dealt with in this way, they tend to resist the lure of unions of supervisors. To public administrators the possibility of such unions is not attractive, but is at least more appealing than bargaining units in which supervisors mix freely with rank and file. The possibilities then of conflicts of interest in handling grievances, or preparing for bargaining, for example, are many. As collective bargaining matures, I would expect growing efforts to pull supervisors out of bargaining units and, following not far behind, a growing number of supervisor unions.

Role of Strike

The role of the strike in government collective bargaining continues to draw both oratory and ingenuity. The doctrinaire positions are relatively simple: One side says that without the strike—or at least the threat to strike—effective collective bargaining cannot take place. In effect, without the bludgeon of a work stoppage the workers have only tender pleas to rely on. The other side argues that strikes against the government are different from those in private industry—they involve unique and vital services and are really strikes against the community. They affirm that stoppages cannot be permitted and that violators should be speedily and effiectively punished.

There are major problems with both positions.

The proponents of the right to strike have to deal with these challenges:

1. There is no need to end the no-strike prohibition. Thousands and thousands of contracts have been and continue to be negotiated in situations where strikes never occur nor were even threatened.
2. To accord the right to strike would be to add to the union's existing—and often exercised—right to push its case through political and legislative channels. An appropriate offset to granting the strike right would be a prohibition on such activity—a higher price than many unions would be willing to pay.
3. The strike is a weapon of doubtful might. In public strikes, the employer actually stands to gain financially, for municipal taxes and fees continue to be levied while the payment of employee salaries is halted (in Newark, New Jersey, it is reported an eleven-week teacher strike cost strikers $2500 each in lost pay but saved the city $7 million). In other areas of substantial unemployment replacements have been hired. In others, even those disputes involving firemen or teachers, "a strike tolerance seems to be developing," according to Robert Howlett, chairman of the Michigan Employment Relations Commission.
4. The opposite view is that granting a right to strike represents potential overkill—the union by withholding vital police, fire, or hospital service can dictate terms to a local government. Citizens cannot purchase these services from a competitor, as in an industrial strike, and the city fathers are therefore sitting ducks.
5. The private sector right to strike model cannot be followed for there the employer has the right to lock out his employees to apply economic pressure. This is not feasible in a public sector dispute.

Those public employers who hold the strike prohibition in awe and affection have some problems, too:

1. Public workers recognize that national labor policy has protected the industrial workers' right to strike for more than three decades. Public workers engaged in driving buses, purifying water, making electricity, or selling liquor feel they should have no lesser rights than the private sector workers who do the same thing.
2. While this is a nation of laws, court action forcing workers to stay on jobs against their will has rarely been effective except in the case of the military draft. And if they choose not to work, penalizing them or their union leaders for striking is not the most efficacious way to start a back-to-work movement. Indeed fines and imprisonment have made martyrs out of union leaders whose tenure may otherwise have been shaky.
3. If the prohibition is to be fair what assurance is there that employers who twiddle their thumbs at the bargaining table comfortably relying on the strike ban can be budged into good faith bargaining?
4. Some contend the argument over the strike right is more oratorical than real anyway. They argue that unions in some states have already won the right in fact, even if not in law, because of court rulings which require employers to show they have bargained in good faith before they

can obtain an injunction and then only when there is proof that an injunction is necessary to prevent "irreparable damage" to public health and safety. These demanding tests, they argue, mean that unions have for practical purposes won a right to strike for a limited period. New legislation enacted in Hawaii and Pennsylvania specifically permits limited strikes after various impasse resolution procedures have been exhausted.

Moves to limit the duration of strikes which break out are based on considerations important to both parties. Strikes are costly—to union treasuries, to the striking employees who face lost pay, and to inconvenienced citizens who suffer and complain and make their suffering known to public officials. Strikes have an uneven effect—for the strong union it may provide such power that the members may have more of a decision over the redistribution of municipal resources than the elected officials, and this is not tolerable for other local employees and taxpayers generally. For a weak union, the legal right to strike may mean a strike has to be played out even though the leaders recognize the end result may be disastrous.

One-day Protests

In addition to withholding services there is another aspect to strikes which has been recognized by out neighbors in Western Europe. Government unions there use the vehicle of the strike to demonstrate—usually only a day or so in order to register their grievances—and in France five days notice is given so that consumers may prepare for the one-day inconvenience. In one case some French employees involved in producing electric power announced they were on strike morally, but stayed on the job keeping the lights burning. The government got the message. It is interesting that in countries where membership of government workers has reached 50 percent and on up to 100 percent, unions choose to employ one-day warnings, or slowdowns, work-to-rule procedures or declination of overtime in order to make their point, rather than unleash their extensive power until their demands are met. They protest but tacitly accept the fact that the government has the last word in setting wages and conditions. Perhaps there is a message for our public unions and public employers here. The short-term cessation of services is a way of educating taxpayers of the value and importance of public service without antagonizing them to the point of retaliation rather than reward.

In this country such messages have also been transmitted by massive sick calls, policemen who report on time but go out only on emergencies, traffic cops who issue no tickets, or in a reverse tactic, traffic policemen who actually and universally enforce a posted twenty-mile-an-hour limit in a city. While such tactics fall short of the inconvenience of a full-fledged strike, they have been effective in calling attention to gripes and grievances, and I believe they will grow in number.

Alternatives

COMPULSORY ARBITRATION

Discussions of public employees' right to strike frequently veer off into evaluations of alternatives. The one eliciting most attention is compulsory arbitration for policemen and firemen, adopted in seven states, or, as in the federal establishment, compulsory arbitration for postal employees. While complaints have been registered from many quarters, my own impression is that the procedure is still on trial, and until we have topped off inflation and the constant chasing of worker salaries to catch up to rising prices, it will not be looked on clinically. There are faults in the system, but some expect too much from a mechanism—for example, some employers looked to arbitrators single-handedly to put the lid on inflationary wage climbing; others on the union side expected the process to crank out awards matching the highest in the nation and at less cost to the union than the bargaining process would have involved. In truth, we do need better arbitrators— ones with courage to return issues to parties because they have not yet really bargained them out in good faith; ones who understand the limitations and restraints of municipal finance as well as they do a private firm's balance sheet; and ones with the sensitivity to recognize, as they do so well in the private sector, what is acceptable and feasible for the parties, as well as just for the employees involved. This is a tall order, but if both parties are required to turn over their important final say on a contract provision to a neutral third party, it is not too much to ask.

There are some procedural mandates that can help the process work and these are likely to be incorporated in developing legislation: both parties should have a choice in the selection of an arbitrator or board of arbitrators; both parties should share the cost of the arbitration equally; issues involved should not endanger survival for either side; issues should be basic and not nebulous and both sides should ac- knowledge a responsibility—in return for the working of the arbitration process—to accept its results.

As things now stand, some critics of the process declare that the only effect of compulsory arbitration is to give unions one more option in the bargaining process—if the arbitrator ups the municipal offer, the union accepts; if he does not, the union strikes, and in a few cases this has happened. On this basis, some city officials look on compulsory ar- bitration as unfair—potentially helpful only to unions and with no compensating advantage to management. In addition, some are so critical of recent wage awards they have indicated they would rather give unions the right to strike, repealing the arbitration statute and regaining the final power to accept or reject an offer for themselves. Just how strongly they would support this if they underwent a widescale police or fire strike or slowdown is open to question. Mayor John V. Lindsay of New York City, who has tasted both, has renewed his demand for final and binding arbitration of such disputes.

In looking at alternatives to strikes one must constantly remember that almost all negotiations wind up in agreements, some faster than others, and that in creating alternatives there is a danger that if they are made too palatable to the parties the end result may well be severe undercutting of a successful bargaining process between parties. In short, one should not try to cure dandruff by cutting off the head.

VARIATIONS

Several variations of the arbitration process have been suggested and may attract followers as practitioners seek substitutes for strikes over contract terms or ways to resolve stoppages once they break out. While compulsory arbitration imposed by state statute may not represent the choice of either party, *voluntary arbitration,* entered into by agreement of the parties, overcomes this objection. Either voluntary or compulsory may be so structured as to require the arbitrator to choose the "best offer" of one side or the other. Theoretically this would push both sides to reasonableness in the hopes that the arbitrator would therefore be more likely to choose their proposal. This process, of course, limits the activity of the arbitrator severely and eliminates the possibility that he can put together a package in which both sides will find at least some comfort. It puts the bargainers in an "all or nothing" posture, but forces the arbitrator to stay within the limits of the offers. A similar, but less confining, arrangement may be possible in which both sides agree to submit the wage award to arbitration with an upper and lower limit and leave other matters in controversy to the best judgment of the arbitrator. Still another variation is to give the arbitrator both sides' best offers on several issues and permit him to put together a package of various "last offers." But none of these results in an agreement fashioned by the joint efforts of the parties— the key advantage of actual bargaining.

In England there is yet another approach which offers promise. Both sides bargain in the customary fashion. At some point they agree to go off-the-record and make concessions in order to settle. If this does not work, however, and the issue goes to arbitration, the offers and positions revert to those previously on-the-record and neither side may make reference to the off-the-record offers. Professor Everett Kassalow of the University of Wisconsin reports it is not unknown for an arbitration tribunal to make an award which a party finds considerably less favorable than its opponent had offered during the informal bargaining stages.

Another possibility is to invoke *arbitration* only after the healing processes of mediation and fact-finding have been applied and one side rejects the fact-finder's recommendations. This is somewhat akin to the New York State experiment with the convening of a show-cause hearing by the legislative body involved in the bargaining so that both sides may publicly air their views on the fact-finder's recommendations and one side attempt to justify its rejection. The New York State Public Employment Relations Board has found that the focusing of a spotlight on recalcitrance and the airing of employee unhappiness about alleged inequities have helped resolve bargaining deadlocks in a substantial percentage of cases. Another New Yorker, Professor Walter E. Oberer of the Cornell University Law School, has offered the suggestion that a strike be considered legal if it follows employer rejection of fact-finder recommendations.

The *"arsenal of weapons"* approach has been supported by several experts as a way of fostering real collective bargaining by keeping negotiators uncertain as to which technique will be used to resolve any deadlocks that might develop. Among the possibilities are mediation, fact-finding, arbitration, or variations of these. The Canadian system under which union bargainers for federal workers declare before the onset of negotiating which route they will follow in case of deadlock has many boosters. The choice open is binding arbitration or strike. Of 114 units, 14 covering 37,000 workers elected the right to strike and the remaining 100 units with 160,000 employees chose arbitration. In actual practice neither route proved very necessary—there were only one strike and four arbitrations in the 114 units. The rest bargained to agreement.

Another approach, derived from industrial experience, is agreement on a *standing umpire,* who will be available in a mediator-arbitrator capacity to assist in resolving deadlocked negotiations, or in deciding grievances which cannot be settled by the parties themselves, and who would generally use his cumulative knowledge of the parties in advancing their labor-management relationship. With his neutrality and yet concern, he may foresee problems coming and could initiate discussions or perhaps research in order to help the parties. He may serve under long-term contract so that emotional responses to his individual actions or decisions may enjoy the healing influence of time and balance.

Also drawn from the private sector success book are such devices as *joint study groups,* which proved their worth in meeting the complex problems arising from substantial automation in the Armour meat packing firm and the Kaiser steel plants, or so-called "continuous bargaining" under which representatives of both parties meet periodically and systematically to discuss mutual problems. These have particular application where the issues involved are so broad and complicated that the thrust and parry of the bargaining table fails to meet the problems.

As such techniques are adopted and perfected parties tend to move away from one-year contracts and the annual "ten months a year we're friends and two months a year we're enemies" cycle into longer-term contracts with safety valves inserted to deal with drastic changes in conditions. Obviously the stabilization of conditions and costs, the avoidance of annual bargaining table squabbles, as well as the savings in negotiating time, energy and dollars, can contribute to better relationships.

PREDICTIONS

Gazing into the crystal ball on which, if any, of these peacemaking procedures will gain in popularity, my guess is that as collective bargaining matures, there will be increasing inclination to experiment with many of these less structured, yet proved, techniques of the private sector when bargaining gets hung up. And new variations or combinations are certain to emerge, catching on or dropping off, as experience indicates.

This process will accelerate to the extent that centralized bargaining takes hold, for many of the devices have special relevancy. Mediation and fact-finding, whether directed by state statute or action of the parties, may be expected to grow and prosper, for here both sides retain their right to accept or reject solutions. Closest to these, voluntary arbitration, the standing umpire, or joint study techniques and other possibilities which while yielding some of the final say yet retain some power.

On the other hand, compulsory arbitration, I believe, has a rocky road ahead. The initial euphoria of the unions about inflation catch-up awards is giving way to some hard-headed appraisals about the high costs of preparing for and carrying out an arbitration proceeding. Also, the breakout of a few strikes after arbitration awards is a reminder that results are not always satisfactory to the public safety forces and a reminder to foes of compulsory arbitration that the process is no guarantee against a strike. Legislators, pressed by a drawn-out strike, may be pushed in this direction occasionally but I doubt there will be general adoption of the mandatory procedure.

Thus far confined to the safety forces of police and fire, compulsory arbitration has been bitterly opposed in the private sector by unions and company alike, for neither likes to give up its power to say yes or no and both recognize the possibility of arbitration pushing real bargaining off the table. If either side believes it can do well in arbitration, and arbitration is available, the tactic to pursue is obvious. Indeed the singling out of municipal safety forces for this special legislative treatment has had some divisive effects on city work forces. The mayor of Dearborn, Michigan, Orville Hubbard, faced with an arbitration award of $291,000 for firemen's raises and retroactive wages, sent individual layoff notices to 56 other city employees, saying, among other things, "The selfish firemen will get bigger paychecks from the city while you get none."

Thus we come to the nagging question, "If strikes by public employees are generally prohibited and if public employers will not see the fairness of their demands, what recourse is left to the workers?" The answer is not simple nor precise, for human relations, particularly as they involve the political process, cannot be dealt with in a mechanistic or exact way. But if we are to retain the no-strike prohibition we must do our utmost to provide effective means for coming as close to justice for employees as they could achieve by withholding their labor.

My view is that collective bargaining in government will expand to the point that most large-size units of government—whether federal, state, county, and city—will be involved. Initially there may be stoppages or slowdowns attributable to the unreality of pent-up, first-time demands by the union or hostility and perhaps inexperience at the bargaining table by either or both parties. But gradually, if the private sector pattern holds true, both sides will get to know one another, understand the other's problems, and look for ways to simplify and expedite the bargaining and such offspring as a regional umpire to help bring parties together, or with the agreement of the parties, actually to decide issues in dispute.

If, however, in a small percentage of cases collective bargaining comes to a dead end, there mediation and fact-finding will continue to dominate impasse resolution as ways of preserving options yet bringing some neutral, hopefully expert, opinion to bear on the parties and the general public as well. If the fact-finder's report is adverse to the public employer's position, the likelihood is that it will be accepted nonetheless, for units of government have found it hard to reject third-party findings. New York City, for example, has so far accepted every fact-finding recommendation substantially. If the recommendations are adverse to the public union's position, the union will be subject to the same pressures of public opinion and may accept.

But whether there is fact-finding or not, the union has the legal right to demonstrate, to make its position known through off-duty informational picketing, newspaper ads, rallies, and the like. And as the numbers of government workers increase and public unions harness this concentration of voters, their potential political clout will assure attention and respect for their position.

The average turnout in municipal elections is only 30 to 50 percent of the registered voters. With the ratio of state and local government workers to total work force approaching one in six, the potential for tipping election results is readily apparent. Indeed a recent survey of state legislatures listed state education associations, which reinforce local teacher bargaining, as among the most effective interest groups in shaping legislation.

Union leaders may lead—or be led—into work stoppages or slow-downs to emphasize dissatisfaction and unhappiness and if these persist it may be necessary to propose ad hoc solutions—arbitration, supermediation, joint study commission, trial periods, or the like.

This is not a clear-cut, precise *modus operandi,* but the alternative of the strike—an economic duel—has so many negative aspects that I doubt it will be generally legalized. It is at once both too strong and too weak—it can paralyze vital services and since these are the monopoly of government there are rarely alternative sources available to the public. Yet on the other hand a strike rarely hurts but rather tends to enhance the economic well-being of the public employer. If the political leadership is willing to take the heat of the inconvenienced public (perhaps cooled somewhat by partial or substitute services), the union has many long weeks of strike benefits to pay out. Governmental strikes have been won—and lost. The record is not one-sided.

Looking down the road, as workers choose unions or associations, strikes will occur and in increasing numbers, often over the lack of adequate ground rules for recognition, frequently over dollars and cents, and sometimes over conditions of special concern to public workers and their employers. We can let worry about strikes dominate the structure of collective bargaining or we can take steps necessary to minimize possible strike causes and provide competent and experienced personnel to help resolve emerging deadlocks before they turn into strikes.

Other Issues

FRINGE BENEFITS

One development in bargaining predictable for the near future is a greater concentration on and greater understanding of fringe benefits. In government, employees have received sick leave, vacations, holidays, retirement, insurance, and other benefits for so long they no longer think of them as part of their wage package—as items which cost public employers money. How expensive is indicated by one city which found that benefits cost about 60 percent of wages for police and firemen and about 40 percent for all other city employees. Similarly, they have grown accustomed to the benefits of the almost automatic wage increases of the step or increment system in most governmental units. Normally, the plan carries employees up the wage ladder as they continue on duty—and costs public employers increasingly larger amounts of money. Negotiations frequently commence with these benefits accepted as money in the bank and go on from there. However, increasingly public employers are identifying the value and cost of these to employees, arguing for example that a 5 percent annual step system and a negotiated 5 percent across the board pay raise add up to a 10 percent pay increase for the affected employee.

From the union's point of view, employers not only have a duty to provide fringe benefits for employees but, because they operate with a broader base, can furnish them much more economically than if employees made individual arrangements. There is a growing emphasis on group life insurance, medical and dental coverage, annual physicals, higher and more portable pensions, longer vacations, and the right to select when to take them.

Improvement of pensions has been a particular target of municipal police and fire forces with the emphasis on fewer years of service and larger proportions of normal pay. Some municipal officers who have made generous concessions in this area have run into criticism from taxpayers' groups that they are saddling future administrations with the cost of paying off the benefits and then have also heard from other municipal employees who demand like treatment. The higher hazard and injury rate of the uniformed personnel has been cited as the main basis for differing treatment, but this is likely to continue as an area of contention not only between parties, but within the ranks of the uniformed services.

ACCOUNTABILITY AND PRODUCTIVITY

Increasing efforts are being made by public managers to induce elements of accountability or productivity into negotiated agreements. One arena has been the school system where parents have complained about Johnny's inability to read or to add. Some have argued for disciplining of teachers whose students fail to demonstrate progress in annual testing. This in turn has led to arguments over relative capability of students and to demands by teachers that if they are to be blamed for a poor product they should have more say in the structuring of the teaching process, including size of class and choice of texts, and in the ordering of needed equipment.

MANDATORY AND PERMISSIVE SUBJECTS

This leads to the old dilemma still haunting the private sector— what items must be bargained about by the parties whether they like it or not, and what are only permissive. Recent efforts in New York State to limit the matters on which unions could require negotiations died in the making. The legislators found that what was one man's managerial prerogative was another's working condition and so left it to the parties to determine initially. The right to assign a social worker a stated quota of welfare cases is an example of such duality.

Some observers believe preparation of lists of mandatory and permissive subjects are fruitless, for a shrewd union negotiator can usually manage a hangup on a mandatory subject until the other side agrees to discuss fully a permissive matter. In short, as one mediator put it, "if the union's got the muscle, they'll talk. If it hasn't, no list will help it." Beyond this is the day-to-day personnel counsel that if a group of employees are hurting, smart employers find ways to listen.

"ABILITY TO PAY"

"Ability to pay" is a phrase increasingly heard at public sector bargaining tables and at arbitrator's hearings and it is easier said, in my opinion, than determined. For some, the problem is a simple one—if employee demands are just, the governmental unit can tax and meet the demands. To others who have delved into the labyrinths of federal-city and state-city relationships, it is enormously complicated. They have run into the thick jungle of statutory restrictions and policy limitations as well as competitive relationships that make "tax and tax, spend and spend" an unrealistic description of municipal powers.

How then does an arbitrator faced with a city's earnest plea of poverty determine whether this is a repeat of some bargaining table cry of "wolf" or the real McCoy? Some have suggested the developing of a tax burden index, which compares the average overall tax and fees burden of a typical resident with the costs facing a typical resident (same salary, size of family, valued home) in comparable communities. This of course would have to be examined in context with statutory limits, debt ceilings, etc., applying to the cities under examination. The drastic outflow of tax-producing residents and jobs from central cities and the influx of low-income, service-needing residents, plus a growing amount of tax-exempt religious, educational, and governmental real estate has severely affected the ability to pay of many cities. Negotiators on both sides, and the public which is to pay the bills, need more insight on such realities.

BLS AND FMCS

The path of collective bargaining can be smoothed, too, by expansion of two federal resources—the Bureau of Labor Statistics and the Federal Mediation and Conciliation Service (FMCS). BLS now furnishes a myriad of useful reports to private sector negotiators, but has only dipped its toes into the public stream. In 1970 a pilot study was begun in eight cities on occupational earnings, work practices, and supplemental benefits in municipal government. Much more is needed. FMCS, which furnishes indispensable service in the private

sector, has hardly come near the public sector water, where its
know-how could be equally helpful. Lack of funds, perhaps more than
policy decisions, seems to have held up expansion of services.

BARGAINING PERSONNEL

Both public unions and public employers will have to expand and
improve their bargaining personnel. Training programs, internships,
institutes, and college courses are on the horizon and growing. In time,
unions and employers may develop a corps of trained labor relations
personnel to handle negotiations and grievances and offer day-to-day
advice on contract administration. Such professionalization can do
much to offset the constant, and perhaps growing, turnover in elected
officials and mobility of career workers. There is no substitute for experience, contacts, and cumulative knowledge in the labor relations
process.

In England the Local Authorities' Conditions of Service Advisory
Board (LACSAB) has provided several hundred municipal employers
with a professional staff which can devote full time to negotiations and
grievances and provide a high degree of skill in dealing with the entire
range of employer-employee relationships. As government unionization
proceeds in this country the LACSAB may prove a valuable model.

It is clear that the larger units of government will need specialists in
labor relations almost immediately. Presently, in the 2100 cities with
populations of 10,000 or more, less than 2 percent have full-time labor
relations officials. The number is growing as chief officers of local government recognize there is as much need for expertise here as in zon-
ing, sewage planning, or other municipal responsibilities and the impact on a city budget can be much greater.

The Future

Looking down the road, not for today or tomorrow, but in the
long run, I believe we will see these patterns unfolding: As employers
adjust to changed relationships, as gross inequities are mended, as employees get a better understanding of their overall benefits, as legislation creates helpful impasse resolution machinery, as the scale of bargaining grows larger, the ratio of strikes to bargaining units will
decline. In many ways the public sector will follow the history, if not
the style, of the private sector, mostly working things out at the bargaining table, but a few disputes will go to the picket line, either because of the depth of feeling over the issue, an internal union situation, an interunion situation, or a clash of the personalities involved.

But where deadlocks occur, I believe the role of the public will be
far greater in the governmental dispute than in the industrial one, for
here the rivalry between the parties is to win the battle for public

opinion. The public employer represents all the citizenry and will take his cue from them. The citizenry will weigh claims carefully because while altruistic fairness may be the uppermost consideration, impact of the settlement on their pocketbooks will not go unconsidered. Public bodies will resort increasingly to fact-finding and similar mechanisms, public unions to educational campaigns through advertisements, and picketing and work actions or stoppages, when they occur, will tend to be short—long enough to get across a protest message to the public employer and the community, but not long enough to become the enduring tests of economic strength typifying major industrial struggles.

A new activist breed of public employees will take over union leadership and the public employer will find labor relations expertise not only desirable but crucial. The labor movement will feel the infusion of an articulate and aggressive constituency, not necessarily unified, however. There is a long distance on the political spectrum from Jerry Wurf's typical AFSCME member to Howard McClennan's fire fighter and perhaps even longer over to the typical federal member in John Griner's AFGE—an employee who sees administrations come and go and adjusts to whoever wins the political duel. The AFL-CIO will be different and yet much the same because as the nine million state and local government people are increasingly unionized and push on the social action front, more of the three million federals will be marching alongside the private sector unions behind the traditional union banner of better wages and more job security.

Change will pervade public sector labor relations for the rest of the seventies and the public employee who takes a year's sabbatical will find many adjustments to be made upon his return. Indeed his union may have won him the option of picking when and where to do his attitude-adjusting and the right to send the bar tab to his employing governmental unit.

The process of collective bargaining is bound to continue growing and experimenting with old paths and developing new ones. The process will require great patience and occasional tension, but will give employees a greater role in the shaping of their own destinies. The infusion of a larger and larger proportion of young people into the government work force is likely to accelerate the process. The 46 percent expansion in the 25- to 34-year age group predicted during the seventies will mean that a lot of the high school and college restlessness and independence will be felt by both government leaders and union leaders. At the same time, as governmental units grow larger and larger, they are faced increasingly with the problems of bringing together labor and management in the common cause of providing a high level of services. Informed and mature collective bargaining can make a contribution in this direction.

Index

178

About The American Assembly

The American Assembly was established by Dwight D. Eisenhower at Columbia University in 1950. It holds nonpartisan meetings and publishes authoritative books to illuminate issues of United States policy.

An affiliate of Columbia, with offices in the Graduate School of Business, the Assembly is a national educational institution incorporated in the State of New York.

The Assembly seeks to provide information, stimulate discussion, and evoke independent conclusions in matters of vital public interest.

AMERICAN ASSEMBLY SESSIONS

At least two national programs are initiated each year. Authorities are retained to write background papers presenting essential data and defining the main issues in each subject.

About sixty men and women representing a broad range of experience, competence, and American leadership meet for several days to discuss the Assembly topic and consider alternatives for national policy.

All Assemblies follow the same procedure. The background papers are sent to participants in advance of the Assembly. The Assembly meets in small groups for four or five lengthy periods. All groups use the same agenda. At the close of these informal sessions, participants adopt in plenary session a final report of findings and recommendations.

Regional, state, and local Assemblies are held following the national session at Arden House. Assemblies have also been held in England, Switzerland, Malaysia, Canada, the Caribbean, South America, Central America, the Philippines, and Japan. Over one hundred institutions have co-sponsored one or more Assemblies.

ARDEN HOUSE

Home of The American Assembly and scene of the national sessions is Arden House, which was given to Columbia University in 1950 by W. Averell Harriman. E. Roland Harriman joined his brother in contributing toward adaptation of the property for conference purposes. The buildings surrounding the land, known as the Harriman Campus of Columbia University, are fifty miles north of New York City.

Arden House is a distinguished conference center. It is self-supporting and operates throughout the year for use by organizations with educational objectives.

AMERICAN ASSEMBLY BOOKS

The background papers for each Assembly program are published in cloth and paperbound editions for use by individuals, libraries, businesses, public agencies, nongovernmental organizations, educational institutions, discussion and service groups. In this way the deliberations of Assembly sessions are continued and extended.

The subjects of Assembly programs to date are:

1951——United States–Western Europe Relationships
1952——Inflation
1953——Economic Security for Americans
1954——The United States' Stake in the United Nations
——The Federal Government Service
1955——United States Agriculture
——The Forty-Eight States
1956——The Representation of the United States Abroad
——The United States and the Far East
1957——International Stability and Progress
——Atoms for Power
1958——The United States and Africa
——United States Monetary Policy
1959——Wages, Prices, Profits, and Productivity
——The United States and Latin America
1960——The Federal Government and Higher Education
——The Secretary of State
——Goals for Americans
1961——Arms Control: Issues for the Public
——Outer Space: Prospects for Man and Society
1962——Automation and Technological Change
——Cultural Affairs and Foreign Relations
1963——The Population Dilemma
——The United States and the Middle East
1964——The United States and Canada
——The Congress and America's Future
1965——The Courts, the Public, and the Law Explosion
——The United States and Japan
1966——State Legislatures in American Politics
——A World of Nuclear Powers?
——The United States and the Philippines
——Challenges to Collective Bargaining
1967——The United States and Eastern Europe
——Ombudsmen for American Government?
1968——Uses of the Seas
——Law in a Changing America
——Overcoming World Hunger